BAD BUSINESS

BAD BUSINESS

*Professional Crime in
Modern Britain*

DICK HOBBS

OXFORD UNIVERSITY PRESS

This book has been printed digitally and produced in a standard specification
in order to ensure its continuing availability

OXFORD
UNIVERSITY PRESS

Great Clarendon Street, Oxford OX2 6DP

Oxford University Press is a department of the University of Oxford.
It furthers the University's objective of excellence in research, scholarship,
and education by publishing worldwide in

Oxford New York

Auckland Bangkok Buenos Aires Cape Town Chennai
Dar es Salaam Delhi Hong Kong Istanbul Karachi Kolkata
Kuala Lumpur Madrid Melbourne Mexico City Mumbai Nairobi
São Paulo Shanghai Taipei Tokyo Toronto

Oxford is a registered trade mark of Oxford University Press
in the UK and in certain other countries

Published in the United States
by Oxford University Press Inc., New York

© Dick Hobbs 1995

The moral rights of the author have been asserted
Database right Oxford University Press (maker)

Reprinted 2003

ISBN 0-19-825848-8

To my parents and to the memory of Jack Reynolds

To Sue, Pat, and Nik

To skulduggery

If drawn by Bus'ness to a Street unknown.
Let the sworn Porter point thee through the Town;
Be sure observe the Signs, for Signs remain,
Like faithful Land-marks to the walking Train.
Seek not from Prentices to learn the Way,
Those fabling Boys will turn thy steps astray;
Ask the grave Tradesman to direct thee right,
He ne'er deceives, but when he profits by't.

(John Gay, *Trivia*)

Acknowledgements

The idea for this book began when several people informed me that my previous work was crap. Both Adrian Maxwell and Snowy the Snout suggested that were I to look at the more serious end of the crime spectrum, some successes could be prised from amongst the dross, and that this is where I should concentrate my future efforts. I am most grateful to both of these good friends for this advice, and for their valuable help throughout the writing of this book.

I wanted to write a book that was accessible both to academics and to a general readership, and Richard Hart, and later John Whelan, at Oxford University Press actively encouraged this. Richard read drafts of two of the early chapters, was always available to talk about the project while I dragged myself through the fieldwork, and really captured the essential essence of the book when on the day that we agreed on an advance, he celebrated by borrowing £10 from me to get a drink. Although I have yet to receive my money back, I have benefited greatly from Richard's good-humoured contributions to the long-winded process of researching and writing this book.

I decided early on to give maximum prominence to the villains' own voices, which meant using a tape-recorder, and my thanks go to Matt Thompson of the BBC for the loan of a machine and most importantly for his help with Chapter 1. I must also acknowledge the late David Cowell, who, when I first had the idea of writing this book, was one of the very few academics in Britain with any scholarly interest in professional crime. Thanks are due to the Nuffield Foundation, and to my employer, Durham University, for providing partial funding of the fieldwork. Many people of a non-villainous tendency have spent time talking to me about this book, or have influenced me as a result of their involvement in some related project. These include Gerry Mars, David Nelken, Gary Armstrong, Clive Norris, Betsy Stanko, Tim Newburn, Sasha Roseneil, Jane Fountain, Penny Green, Stuart Chilvers, Mike Ahearn, Steve Hall, and, as ever, Paul Crace, the Prince of Shoreditch. I must also never forget Preston Thomas, Rod Hudson, Terry Hunt, Mickey Childs, Steve Sawkins, Jimmy Harris, Phil Limber, Ray Gibbs, John Goodman, and all the other ghosts of Plaistow to whom I owe more than a drink. Likewise to Malcolm Read, who when my computer malfunctioned administered an enema to the machine and retrieved and helped reassemble the text.

Steven Parrot ran two invaluable one-day conferences on organized crime at Birkbeck College, which were the most enjoyable, non-competitive academic events that I have ever attended. As a result of these conferences I gained much, partly from the papers that were presented, but mainly from subsequent conversations with John Lea, Roger Lewis, Graham Saltmarsh, Vincenzo Ruggerio,

Paddy Rawlinson, and Walter Easy. Thanks are also due to Kevin Stenson, who I see no more than a couple of times a year, but from whose commitment to both street ethnography and Freddy King I always glean much.

Not for the first time David Downes, Nigel Fielding, and Terry Morris did the right thing. Similarly both Geoff Pearson, who has always been supportive, and retains the invaluable ability to find something extraordinary in his local pub, and Richard Wright, who spent a year at Durham while he was writing up his burglary study. Their enthusiasm for ethnographic work with active criminals, at a time when so many academics are devoting their time to producing repair manuals for the criminal justice system, has been infectious. A few snippets of conversation have acquired significance. Something Richard Sparks said about methods, Robert Reiner said about what people want to read, Neil Shover said about street ethics and academic ethics, and Rod Morgan said about children eating cornflakes, have all rattled around in my mind for some time. Graham 'the truth' Hurley told me precisely that, and Dave Hooper dealt with the media and blagged a top-of-the-range Ford Scorpio. Tim May read more of the early drafts of Chapter 4 than is healthy, and I always found his comments helpful. Bob Lilly provided me with a comprehensive clippings' file on John Gotti, with weekly news from 'Jerry's Jug House', and made me laugh a lot.

Most importantly, I am very lucky to be working in an environment that is incredibly supportive. I am most grateful to all members of the Department of Sociology and Social Policy at Durham. To Margaret Bell for typing and helping with the manuscript, and Sarah Goff for transcribing and typing. In particular, Robin Williams, David Chaney, Nick Ellison, Bob Roshier, Dave Byrne, Ian Roberts, and Richard Brown have created a really pleasant atmosphere in which to work. Books, articles, videos, jokes, everything, thank God, but the administrative workload is shared in an atmosphere of vicious good humour.

At this stage it is customary for authors to pay homage to their family, and to acknowledge the suffering inflicted upon them by the process of researching and writing their latest tome. Sad to report that apparently my family did not suffer. The absences from home were a bit inconvenient, but they got on with their business, and the advance that I received paid for a holiday. The things that I am grateful to my family for are nothing to do with work, and this book was work.

However, writing this book did seem to have some strange effects on my children. My 6-year-old son started to talk about the dangers of drugs, in particular 'taking crap', while the 9-year-old became increasingly fascinated by the cryptic telephone messages that he took, particularly from 'Snowy the Snout'. If in the future there does prove to be any long-lasting psychological damage, they should be grateful that their father was not a practising —— (readers can fill in the gap according to their own prejudices).

Finally, I am grateful to all those informants that gave up their time to help me with this book. The manner in which they make their living may inspire bouts of moral indignation in some readers, but none of the criminals featured in this book received any payment from me. Their lives have not been glamorized, and I have sought to avoid idealizing crime. Theirs is a bad business and this book is an attempt to understand it.

Contents

Introduction

This book is concerned with active criminals, most of whom at the time of writing are 'well at it'. It is an attempt to engage with their culture.

Professional crime is a subject whose definition few people can agree upon. Who can legitimately claim to be a professional criminal? The 14-year-old who commits hundreds of burglaries to support his addiction to video games? The car thief who moves from joy-riding to supplying a team of car-ringers? What about the kid in the mock Armani suit with the stolen mobile phone *sans* batteries; is he a drug-dealer or a sad bastard with an image problem?

Yet, commonsensically, few of us would fail to recognize the teams of armed robbers who were so successful during the late 1960s and early 1970s as anything other than professional;[1] similarly, the safe-cracker of the 1950s, or the contemporary drug-importer. These people are anything but part-time amateurs. But what about those committed to crime as a way of life, as a means of earning a living or of establishing some cultural clout in a harsh world of declining legitimate opportunities? Is it the nature of the crime, the consistency of the criminal, or the competence with which the crime is committed that leads us to use the term 'professional'? This definitional ambiguity should not detract from the centrality of the concept of professional crime, nor from its essential vitality. Indeed, it is this very ambiguity that triggers cynical recognition as we establish ironic connotations, suggesting a life-world parallel to, and reflective of, normative society.

This *frisson* of recognition of forms of behaviour that are all too often hidden from scholarly gaze by the hypocrisy of legal imperatives, and ignorance masquerading as moral outrage is craftily exploited by the entertainment industry, and by the writers who prodigiously stock the shelves of the True Crime section of our local bookstore. We tend to lean heavily upon these accounts for our images of serious crime. For as science fiction has been so influential in shaping our visions of alternative worlds and distant galaxies, so crime fiction, television, and film mould our perceptions of the serious end of the crime spectrum.

There has been a lack, particularly in Britain, of academic attention paid to serious crime. Research on juvenile criminals, victims, policing, in addition to a whole gamut of essentially administrative concerns, written from a range of political perspectives, dominate the agenda as we are encouraged to join the fight against crime, sometimes at the expense of basic academic curiosity. Agendas are increasingly set by agencies charged with funding by government, either directly or indirectly. However, current reluctance to engage with deviant groups stems only in part from the reasonable assertion that categories such as professional criminality are by definition problematic to locate and analyse. Bourgeois squeamishness about developing a level of empathy with deviant groups in the light of political exhortations to 'walk with a purpose' and be 'tough on crime' does the rest.

Researching this subject is of course both practically and ethically difficult, just like real life. Active criminals in particular have little to gain from exposing their practices to the pauperized milksop gaze of an academic. Yet numerous writers have succeeded in engaging with deviant populations through some variant upon ethnographer–participant observation, and appreciation of the pragmatic conundrums that can arise from such studies and recognition of the theoretical strategies that underpin them is vital.[2] However, a detailed analysis of the utility of these research tools as part of a study of professional crime will not be a feature of this book. Such analyses have a habit of lapsing into apologetic justifications of a technique that, no matter what is written, will be criticized by those of alternative methodological and theoretical dispositions.[3] I whole-heartedly concur with Mike Levi's view that 'I would rather receive a bad academic review, however unmerited, than have my face smashed in'.[4] This book is concerned with a world where the latter is a distinct possibility, and as a consequence the former becomes rather less intimidating than some gladiators of the academy might suppose. Therefore, I have risked flaunting academic orthodoxy by postponing a detailed methodological discussion of the problems of researching covert deviant populations for a proposed journal article.[5]

Not wishing to focus upon any single criminal or legalistic category, I selected an ethnographic study of professional criminals as the primary strategy for this book in an attempt to tease out the boring everyday strategies that committed serious criminals employ as part of their daily grind. Contentious information was cross-checked with informants, friends, families, and colleagues. Local newspapers were useful in verifying factual material, and friendly journalists and police officers were occasionally invaluable (only the former attempted to call in their debts).

The research upon which this book is based involved engaging with criminals in their pubs, clubs, offices, and homes; on their terms, using their language. It is important to stress that to research criminals does not indicate a permanent change of address;[6] indeed I started this study by acknowledging that this was their world, and that I had no intention of staying.[7] But if criminal decision-making and the consequent culture 'is to be situated in the wider context of their day to day existence, an existence dominated by the temptations and pressures of life on the street',[8] the researcher must at least be prepared to make the journey.

Desperate to avoid the attitude parodied by Polsky that 'the only real criminal is a caught criminal',[9] I have endeavoured wherever possible to engage with professional criminals 'au natural, in the field . . . as they normally go about their work and play . . . uncaught criminals and the study of others who in the past have been caught but are not caught at the time you study them'.[10]

Indeed if criminals are studied when they are no longer active, there is a real danger that the study of, for instance, the inmates of prisons may produce studies of prison inmates.[11] As Solway and Waters have indicated in a discussion concerned with fieldwork among heroin addicts, 'If addicts are studied in jail, the result is a study of prisoners. If the ethnographer's goal is to understand addiction, he must resolve himself to entering the natural habitat of the addict, the streets, the back alleys, the shooting galleries.'[12]

However, if the research demands large samples of criminals who have engaged in a specific criminal activity, then resort to the penal system is inevitable.[13] That is not the aim of this study, which is concerned more with the personal and social arrangements of professional crime than with obtaining a sample of criminals within a common legal category who happen to be sharing the experience of incarceration. Indeed it became apparent during the course of this study that most serious criminals when they are put in prison are seldom locked up for engaging in their principal, that is occupationally defined, activity. Burglars are arrested for fraud, bank-robbers for assault, non-specialists for absolutely any offence. Due to the chaotic lives of many serious criminals, drink, drugs, driving offences, debt, and petty violence often feature prominently on their CVs, while seldom affecting their master status, which is derived from their primary economic activity.

Chambliss suggests that 'All we really have to do is to get out of our offices and onto the street',[14] but this frankly romantic view, heavily scented with Robert Park's exhortations to his students to engage in the noble cause of fieldwork,[15] does little to instruct the reader how to go about conducting research on a population which is defined by straight society according to its ability to maintain covert status. Further, it makes certain assumptions about the social competence of researchers. Fleisher puts the problem into a nutshell: 'Many scholars who discuss and analyse the lives and beliefs of criminals, including prisoners, haven't spent enough time on the street and in prisons among their subjects to understand the cultural and semantic context of their speech. To use a linguistic analogy, outside researchers often report the phonetics of crime without understanding its syntax and semantics'.[16]

The other problem is that criminals do lie. A television company employed me as a consultant on a programme about 'the underworld', and after much cajoling I agreed to find them an active criminal. This was to be a one-off for them, as all the other villains in the series were extremely long in the tooth, were serving lengthy sentences, or had retired from crime in order to take up autobiography. The TV personnel met my contact on several occasions, and each time he behaved outrageously, running in and out of pubs in Soho claiming that he was being followed, arranging to meet a researcher at a Matisse exhibition and lecturing her on the finer points of the artist's work, cancelling appointments at the last minute as he had urgent business abroad, and finally having the audacity to refuse the programme-makers' demand to provide his real name so that they could check his authenticity. (With who? Central Casting?). The programme-makers then telephoned me to complain about his behaviour, and I explained that this man, a successful thief and drug-dealer, had behaved just like a criminal.

Wright and Decker were keen to deal with problems of deceit and mischief, by applying a unique tactic in employing an ex-offender as a contact with the street people that they hoped to interview.[17] The results as demonstrated in their study of burglars displays a deep understanding of the criminals' perspective, indicating that the day-to-day tribulations of 'life on the street' are part of, not separate from, criminal action.

An alternative to either prison research or ethnography is to enter Jurassic Park and play with the dinosaurs. Criminal biographies and autobiographies represent excellent source material for any researcher,[18] and they are used liberally in this book.[19] Yet total reliance upon accounts of ex-criminals, as they recount halcyon days of honourable gore and filthy lucre, is dangerous. Deception is part of the criminal game, yet it is upon these often cosy elderly-male reminiscences of blags, shags, and sawn-offs, in a fog-bound Ealing-comedy post-war Britain, where ritual slaughter and American saloon cars merge seamlessly with full employment and outside privies, that our vision of the British underworld has been constructed.[20]

Professional crime was largely disregarded by academics until the University of Chicago's Department of Sociology initiated a shift towards sociological studies of aspects of urban life that had previously been ignored.[21] The received version of the Chicago school's methodological stance is that of a 'special emphasis on firsthand acquaintance with social life',[22] yet there is considerable evidence suggesting that this rendition of the Chicagoan model is at best romantic.[23] The contradictory and cross-disciplinary aspects of the Department's work, as Platt indicates,[24] has somewhat muddied the myth, yet studies of low life were now regarded as academically feasible. However, the Chicago school's general theoretical tendencies were inclined towards a framework that appears to contradict the vast wealth of empirical material that constituted the Department's typical output. Social disorganization was regarded as the primary dynamic that inspired criminal action, and was deemed to be caused by a lack of both formal and informal controls within a community.[25]

Sutherland's *The Professional Thief*[26] is a landmark in criminological research for a number of crucial reasons. Co-written with Chic Conwell, a professional thief, Sutherland provides a key rendition of a form of criminality that is impossible to define or identify by any criteria that originate in legalistic constructions of criminal action. Further, for Sutherland, professional crime is a fragment of criminal activity to be comprehended as a separate behaviour system[27] organized around theft. Sutherland ignored legal diktats, concentrating upon cultural identity, and therefore offered an alternative to the dominant Chicagoan explanation of crime as being the result of social disorganization.[28] Sutherland suggests a behaviour system that features characteristics of technical skill, consensus via a shared ideology, differential association, status, and, most importantly, informal organization.

Sutherland's unequivocally sociological theory has found considerable support in subsequent empirical work.[29] However, the highly volatile nature of the market-place has conspired to manufacture a social environment within which Sutherland's highly structured concept of professional crime is hotly contested. For instance, Lemert[30] presents cheque-forgers as loners of negligible skills, while the President's Commission[31] stresses the importance of 'hustlers' who are adaptable, non-specialist, all-purpose criminals, and who do not exhibit consensus with other hustlers, therefore calling in question the notion of a cohesive behaviour system as suggested by Sutherland.

Indeed it is the idea of the status of high-status specialist and the subsequent subcultural formations of criminal specialisms that have provoked the bulk of criticism of Sutherland's work amongst empirically orientated criminologists. For example, Letkemann uses the term 'rounders' to describe the all-purpose adaptive criminal.[32] Yet he also emphasized that an explicit commitment to criminal activity as a means of making a living provided the best criterion for differentiating between professional and non-professional offenders. Consequently, Sutherland's model is not entirely discounted by Letkemann, who displays some support for the notion of an occupational group defined by its level of commitment to illegal economic activities.

The most useful and historically relevant segment of Sutherland's theory remains the notion of full-time commitment to crime as a pragmatic starting-point for the study of what Block, in an effort to demystify organized crime, has defined as the 'serious crime community'.[33] The dissection of Sutherland's theory was continued by Einstadter, who explored the subcultural possibilities that emerge when a group of specialists share this criminal commitment.[34] Although consistency of practice and a measure of ideological coherence were discovered, Einstadter found that contrary to Sutherland's theory, armed robbers were not reliant upon a system of tutelage, nor did they maintain relationships with quasi-legitimate agents such as fences, who are able to maintain one foot in the straight world.

Although one can imagine armed robbers who target hard currency not requiring the services of commercial intermediaries, for the bulk of thieves a cipher into the legitimate world with the ability to turn loot into cash is crucial. Therefore, it is vital when attempting to comprehend professional criminal practice to include what Mack and Kerner have called 'background operators',[35] who through their quasi-legal status create frameworks of legitimacy upon which the professional criminal might build a consistent and enduring practice. Mack and Kerner point out that our understanding of professional crime is dominated by a misdirected concentration upon 'The front line operators . . . the house breakers or the van or bank robbers, or the hijackers or fraudsters'.[36] As a consequence, two vital categories are ignored: the 'service-providers' and, most importantly, the 'background organizers'. Mack and Kerner proceed to claim that the high status of the front-line operator is false, and that we should be focusing upon the organization behind the front-liners.

Indeed, the dealer in stolen goods is pivotal to the competent and efficient functioning of any professional thief. Several writers situate the trade in stolen goods within a milieu that is dominated by the mores of mainstream economic activity.[37] Our attention is then shifted from a subterranean universe of dark deeds and evil intent to focus upon the commonplace ambiguities to be found in the commercial overworld.

Shover has established that the social organization of burglary is closer to the classic analysis of Sutherland than that of the cheque-forger or the armed robber,[38] as implied by Lemert and Einstadter respectively. However, Shover proposes that it is the exigencies of burglary that necessitate the creation of networks of dependency, rather than, as Sutherland suggests, an essentially subcultural bonding based upon shared occupational status. Additionally, Shover acknowledges that these networks will continue to evolve as a result of changes in policing, security, and technology.

In this book the all-purpose, non-specialist criminal, the rounder or hustler,[39] will be afforded considerable attention. For as the concept of the market grows in importance within both criminal and non-criminal spheres, the labour force fragments into flexible coalitions of similarly economically disposed individuals. Crucially for those engaged in criminal action, the temporary nature of occupational coalitions is ensured by the essentially erratic character of market forces, and by the considerable advantage to be gained from an ever-changing workplace and *modus operandi*.

The mobility and flexibility that is the mark of contemporary professional criminals has been accompanied by a perception amongst retired villains, police officers, and writers that there has been a decline in the moral standards upon which it is claimed the identity and solidarity of professional criminals were once constituted.[40] As in the straight world there is a constant harking back to a golden age of predictability, stoicism, honour, and reliability.[41] It is apparent, therefore, that professional criminals of a certain age are as prone to bouts of nostalgia as any other individual. They yearn for stability, and a mythical age when justice, albeit rough, provided righteous justifications for their villainy that stand in vivid contrast to the amorphous nature of contemporary crime, with its commercial rather than ethical frontiers.

The unwritten criminal code that charts a set of ethics providing a framework for a sharply delineated community of professional criminals is a powerful and pervasive concept that succeeds in drawing parallels with conventional professional communities. This concept draws heavily upon Sutherland's original template of a coherent group which has 'a complex of abilities and skills, just as do physicians, lawyers or bricklayers'.[42]

Some of the most powerful claims for a self-contained code of ethics held by professional criminals are to be found in studies of prison subcultures. It is claimed by both Irwin, and Irwin and Cressey that the most crucial aspect in determining an inmate's adaptation to incarceration is the culture that accompanies him to the institution.[43] Further, it is claimed that the culture of the professional criminal is easily adapted to prison regimes, for the identity of criminal is one that carries currency both inside and outside the context of institutional confinement. Currency is particularly attributed to qualities of 'rightness' and 'solidness', and attributes of 'honesty', 'responsibility', and 'loyalty'. It is vital for the criminal to 'meet his obligations, pay his debts, keep his appointments, and most importantly never divulge information to anyone which may lead to the arrest of another person. His character, his "rightness", is one of the most important dimensions of his life'.[44] The credibility of former identities is enhanced rather than erased, and the professional's commitment to a criminal identity is an important component in an individual's adaptation to prison, confirming that prison is a constituent element of the larger criminal culture.[45]

However, the code of the professional criminal appears to 'free world' researchers to be little more than a rhetorical device that functions in the face of a constantly changing working environment and ever-fluctuating personnel to maintain artificially some sense of exclusive status.[46] As a report from the mid-1960s states, 'The shifting, transitory pattern of most professional criminals' working relationships was found to be accompanied by the absence of any strong ethical codes'.[47]

A professional code of ethics may have been a feasible concept when the relevant organizations and technologies of professional crime required an ethical base as an instrumental foundation for competent practice, for instance as an exchange for information. However, as can be observed from an analysis of armed robbery in Britain in the 1970s, when informants, security measures, and police tactics combined to render these practices redundant, the criminal code is judiciously ousted by a rhetoric somewhat less than 'righteous', yet easily recognized by those more accustomed to the self-justifications of legitimate economic activity.[48] The professional criminals that I encountered while researching this book were overwhelmingly ambivalent about any coherent ethical framework.

In terms of drawing a direct analogy with the legitimate economic order, skill,[49] craft,[50] and competence,[51] the everyday methodologies inherent in the committal of crime as work[52] are likely to prove the most productive. These qualities are crucial in establishing occupational competence, and defining competent criminal performance is central to Luckenbill's study of armed robbery.[53] The crucial problem for the robber is 'How do I gain and maintain compliance from my victims?' In Luckenbill's study, robbery is considered as a set of transactions that are articulated and managed by the robber, and implicate both the robber and his victims in the accomplishment of four interrelated tasks: the robber establishes his presence with the victim, the interaction is immediately transformed into 'the robbery frame', the prize is handed over to the robber, and finally the robber leaves the scene. The enabling device for the successful completion of these four stages is coercion based on the threat of physical force.[54]

Economic rationality is a relatively simple way of dealing with both forms of property crime and, as will become apparent below, the new service industry that is built around drugs. Violence at the professional level is somewhat more complex, and even though this book does not deal empirically with the extremes of professional violence, the world of the professional killer as uniquely introduced by Levi offers some valuable methodological and theoretical insights.[55] Using frame analysis, Levi's study is about the personal management of deviance, and the neutralization through 'reframing' of a criminal activity that is unlikely to find its professional status contested. Professional murderers, unlike professional thieves, are able, by virtue of the rarity of their specialism, to establish a rarefied niche within the labour market. Further, through reframing the victim as a target, and receiving payment for his services, the professional murderer not only avoids self-stigmatization, but also enhances the status of murderer to that of a supremely rational market operative. The hit man commercializes an impersonal level of violence; he is the consummate professional, a commodifier of death.

The exclusive milieu of the professional criminal has been breached by the barbarism of enterprise cultures, and as a consequence it is the culture of normative commercial practice that provides the template for the practices of 'full-time miscreants'.[56] Conventional approaches such as Mack's, due to their capacity to consider the relationship between professional crime and working-class entrepreneurships generating culture, remain valuable. Yet they should be reinforced not only by studies that highlight the instrumental ambiguity of much contemporary criminal enterprise[57] and those concerned with its relationship to the economic and ideological frameworks that sustain it,[58] but also by studies that emphasize the symbiotic relationship that exists between members of serious-crime networks and those who are charged by society with their control.[59]

The cultures that have traditionally nurtured professional crime now feature variations on inherited conventional engagement with the money economy that reflect the range of activities that constitute expert explorations of recently evolved markets.[60] While some of these settings reflect many of its practitioners' traditional schooling in rough places,[61] the work of Block and Levi suggests that we can no longer distinguish crime from normal business.[62] 'Much crime does not fit into a separate category. It is primarily a business activity.'[63]

Fraud and the drug trade in particular constitute generic engagements with the market-place that suggest the merging of 'upper and underworld'.[64] Structural alterations to the market-place, such as the deregulation of the London Stock Exchange in 1986, and key technological innovations, particularly in the field of electronic communications,[65] have enabled those of villainous intent to launch offensives upon information, or money, when and where it is most vulnerable that are comparable to the way that the shotgun and the thermic lance enabled and enhanced the practice of previous generations of thieves and robbers.[66]

The essential ambiguity between criminal and legal commercial action is best expressed by those writers concerned with the drugs trade.[67] The scope and variety offered by drug-dealing to those seeking to explore criminal entrepreneurial possibilities are considerable, and the similarities between drug-dealing and legitimate business highlight yet again the problem of using the term 'professional crime' in relation to an exclusive cultural and occupational space. The problems inherent in attempting to develop criminal typifications within a market-place that, despite being dominated by a single commodity, is as fragmented by class, race, and gender as any legitimate economic sphere can be examined by looking at the work of Ruggeiro, and Adler and Adler.[68] Drug economies are not homogeneous, and success or failure will inevitably be relative concepts for operatives engaging with markets that vary greatly in terms of refinement and intensity.[69]

Professional dealers who are able to sustain successful businesses will seek to invest in legal enterprises, and the lack of opportunities for such investment both within ghetto cultures[70] and in the context of static economic regimes,[71] certainly compared to those of élite drug markets,[72] is likely to curtail the prospect of longevity, and therefore reduce the chance of skill, consensus, shared ideology, and most crucially organization being allowed to bloom. Further, criminal organizations have histories that will provide foundations upon which new structures can emerge. Indeed this particular archaeology of knowledge can provide clues to the genesis of professional criminal formations that demolish the big bang theory that is at the heart of notions of criminal pathology.[73]

Ethnic and cultural adaptations to economic and legal fluctuations are not the only variations upon the economic rationality that this book claims is the motivating force of much professional criminal activity. As Katz has established,[74] and this book will seek to elaborate, other motivational factors come into play when attempting to establish the *raison d'être* of criminal actors. Not least of these is hedonism. Criminals enjoying their work and working to enjoy their leisure are not insignificant issues if we are to understand the culture that nurtures and sculpts professional crime. Yet this is not to suggest that there is some vast gulf between instrumental and non-instrumental crime, for the market-place can, certainly in the case of drugs, create an environment that will enable both entrepreneurial and hedonistic engagement.

What has been traditionally defined as professional crime has now fragmented into a number of quite distinctive forms of criminality. The decline of key criminal activities that were previously central to the concept of professional crime into haphazard, essentially amateur excursions[75] featuring minimal planning, a low level of competence, and a lack of commitment to specialized criminality[76] typifies contemporary armed robbery and stands in stark contrast to the teams of robbers whose competent practice was efficient enough to establish 'blaggers' as a criminal élite.[77]

The armed robber has been succeeded by a far more ambiguous figure. The adoption of entrepreneurship as a central ideological prop of post-traditional society has initiated a consolidation of legitimate and illegitimate interests around a central theme of wealth accumulation.[78] The principal consequence of this alliance is that the term 'professional criminal' now carries with it an ambiguity that is entirely appropriate to a post-traditional order that shuns preconceived class-based notions of structural and ideological constraint. In turn these notions are inextricably linked to social forms that were the direct product of a division of labour which in late twentieth-century capitalism shows every sign of obsolescence. However, as professional criminals have established their cultural authority within orthodox frameworks, they are better equipped than most to adapt to the new economic order. Accordingly, the shift by professional criminals towards entrepreneurial activities is indicative of the reproduction of normative, post-traditional economic relations within the convoluted contours of illegitimate markets.

Contemporary professional criminals *are* businessmen; there is no nod and a wink toward cheeky-chappie incongruity; they are not pretending any more; they merely buy and sell commodities in accord with market principles. Outrageous savagery seldom constitutes a finale. Violent episodes are necessary facets of both local and international trade, and are usually perpetrated at the points of production or consumption. Competent practitioners are as removed from a bomb massacre in Medellin, or the shooting of a bouncer in Wallsend, as an executive in a multinational tobacco company is from a cancer ward in Hackney.

Professional criminals in this book, while obviously conversant with the day-to-day trials and tribulations of their business, seldom expressed a concern with the wider contexts of their practice beyond their immediate enacted environment. They were as restricted and narrow-minded about their work as most non-criminals are about their respective occupations. Few chemical-plant workers are willing to discuss the long-term effects of their industry on the environment, or fast-food operatives the implications of their product on the nation's health. Beyond economic instrumentality, albeit informed with a variety of rhetorical provisos that set the outer parameters of their practice, professional criminals are unlikely to consider the contextual frameworks and structural arrangements that enable their work to continue. The exceptions are those pros who have been forced into semi- or full retirement by combinations of old age and the criminal justice system.[79] They have had the time and enforced leisure to contemplate their careers, and are often dismayed at what they perceive as a decline in the moral fabric of the criminal fraternity. When professional criminal Eric Mason reacquainted himself with gaol after a number of years on the outside he found

an entirely different type of criminal from the men I had found it worth suffering with, years before. . . . I was disgusted by the complete disregard shown by the majority of inmates for the misery that they had caused their victims, and the pleasure they got from relating stories showing the despicable habits of common house-breakers like themselves. . . . I would remember my first years in prison when the common housebreaker, muggers of old people and ponces, those that lived off the immoral earnings of prostitution, were only considered to be just one step above the child molesters; they knew it and were very loath to talk about their crimes.[80]

Crime flies, and if the prison population, or at least prison subculture, has altered, then so too has the nature of élite professional criminals. There has emerged a highly flexible professional with the abilities and resources to engage in a myriad of entrepreneurial activities. The commitment that is displayed by these individuals is not to a subculture, or occupational group, but to the prime motivational ethos of 'economic man',[81] the acquisition of wealth.[82] Their competence in engaging with and manipulating markets is increasingly similar to the strategies and *modus operandi* of legitimate traders.

As will become apparent, this engagement with illegal markets, using normative commercial strategies, can introduce the professional criminal to the possibilities of the legitimate market-place, blurring still further the distinction between criminal and non-criminal entrepreneurship, and highlighting the essential essences that lie at the core of commerce. The informal and constantly renegotiated division of labour within professional criminality assures that this élite group, through its control of relevant markets, is able to establish elements of continuity and stability that can in every sense be described as 'organized'.

Certainly in relation to British organized crime, it is apparent that each criminal activity generates, and is reliant upon, organizational structures that are unique to that activity. Consequently, in the absence of traditional hierarchically based Sicilian–American organized crime,[83] British professional criminals have developed from well-established configurations of acquaintances and family to *ad hoc* coalitions that can be adapted to the exigencies of the contemporary market, with 'alliances and networks flow[ing] from their exceptionally flexible frame'.[84] These microstructures generate their own identities that are often rooted in historical precedent, and competition is as likely to erupt as a result of ancient territorial feuds as over market dominance.

Because of the transformation to entrepreneurial criminality, overlaps with other criminological categories are unavoidable, and such idiosyncratic domains as white-collar, professional, corporate, or organized may become problematic if they are studied as separate isolated phenomena. However, despite the ambiguous terminology that pervades the study of this level of criminality, it will become apparent in subsequent chapters that the cultural chrysalis from which many professional criminals emerge shows a remarkable continuity with the past.

In one of the few relevant British studies that seeks to locate the enabling culture that nurtures professional criminality, Mack adopted a conventional class-orientated subcultural stance.[85] Mack concentrates upon the role of the traditional base from which most 'full-time miscreants' emerge, and focuses upon the crucial role of competence in the maintenance of networks, which in turn lend structure to serious criminal activity. However, as will become obvious from the range of individuals and activities referred to in subsequent chapters, if we are to advance our understanding of professional criminality, our definitions of what constitutes criminal competence need to be as flexible as the market-place itself. What is required is a definition that locates competent practice and expert status, rather than one that responds to legal edicts or to the myths that are promulgated by popular culture.[86]

The term 'professional crime' is therefore far from anachronistic.[87] It resonates across generations with the tone of our social and economic lives, merely requiring occasional returning in accord both with changing opportunity structures and with the consequent ideological reseating that marks the states of flux which are prime characteristics of modern societies.

1
Apprentices to Dealers

THE CRAFTSMAN. All of us, I think, we were born too late. I think if we were born 200 years ago we'd have been pirates. . . . You open a safe and you think this is the one, then you open another one but this has got to be the one. It's like the old gold prospector, he keeps digging and digging to see what he finds, and you'll find that a lot of criminals are very persistent people—they'll keep at it.

THE THIEF. When it came to working I was learning how to make money from nothing, and you don't get that from the ordinary people, so you find them who are like you, and just find that the others who are at it are the only ones who know.

THE DEALER. It's very appealing—very appealing. I mean I know people who dedicate their lives to being the smackiest smack addict ever because they just get into it, they love that sort of horrible smackie nasty smackhead—I do have a lot of problem with that because I just can't stand people—they're incredibly boring and they're just pathetic.

In this book I will claim that professional criminals are part of an occupational continuum that spans the centuries. Like any other profession, if it is to survive it must adapt, and consequently specific forms of professional crime will now seem as arcane as lamplighters and knockers-up seem to those of us fortunate enough to enjoy electricity and alarm clocks. Technological innovation, alterations in business practice, and shifts in demand have resulted in the deskilling or market decimation of great swathes of the workforce, and as a consequence shipbuilders and dockers are now as rare as safe-crackers and professional armed robbers.

Professional crime evolves in tandem with the dominant practices of the legitimate economic order. We can chart this evolution by analysing the case histories of a craftsman, an artisan, and an entrepreneur, whose working lives parallel chief concerns and dominant identities of the last fifty years.

Professional criminals do it for money. They plunder cash and property, trade in illegal substances, and seldom feel any compulsion to pay National Insurance contributions or donate any portion of their loot to the Inland Revenue. They are outside the law but inside society.

This chapter is about the working lives of three professional criminals. Their careers span five decades and a wide range of strategies and techniques. However, in order to appreciate and fully understand their work it is necessary to resist the temptation to blow the moral whistle on their enterprise. If outrage is suspended, lives of some richness will emerge—lives dedicated to making money from crime. The most outstanding characteristic common to all three is the utter normality of their explanations and justifications. For they live in the same world as us: they have families, they worry about the future, and, most importantly, they have to cope with a rapidly changing world that can suddenly make skills that took years to acquire totally obsolete.

THE CRAFTSMAN

This is what happened to master craftsman Dick Pooley. He dedicated most of his life to criminal pursuits and now in his sixties has a comfortable life with few regrets. Dick Pooley is a safe-cracker, and was introduced to safe-breaking by his elder brother, but it was only after he was caught and imprisoned that he learnt to take his trade seriously.

My brother, who's a couple of years older than me, showed me how to open a safe. He used to do safes himself, and we used to manhandle them and take the blacks off—it was so easy. In fact, I timed myself once on a clock in this particular place and we took the back off in twenty minutes—a safe, a big safe, and we got right in and there was nothing in it. So we cast around and found the money in a gas oven—they'd put it in the gas oven. (Laughs.)
  So I learned how to open a safe and quick, with the less noise. And I went to gaol and I was put in a cell in Wandsworth, and I meet a man who was probably one of the best safe-blowers in London, and his name—he's dead now—his name was—they called him the Silver Fox of Camden Town, and his name was Alan Robinson. A big, big man and he was one of Billy Hill's boys and done a lot of villainy in his time—guns and all the rest of it, but earned quite a bit of money. He took me to a place in New Cross and he loaded a safe up, so I watched him do it. We came out of the room to set the charge off and it didn't work, so we tried wiring it up to different electrical gadgets . . . and it still wouldn't work, so Alan said to me 'Go and have a look and see why it's not working.' So I walked up to the safe and I wriggled the detonator about, little knowing that it could have killed me stone dead.
  There was three of us. Alan must have been in his sixties, the other man was in his seventies—an old age pensioner he was. I always remember him saying to me 'Dick do you mind if I don't come up the stairs? If it comes on top I won't be able to get away.' I said 'You stay there,' so he stayed there, and we went up and done the business, got the money, and come down, helped the pensioner over the wall—but they're dead now and they're great people.

An essential part of Pooley's apprenticeship involved gaining access to raw materials, and he quickly displayed early signs of a virtuoso temperament, even while acquiring the basics of his craft.

Other people in the criminal fraternity wouldn't have anything to do with us 'cos they thought we was mad—and we were mad, looking back. We used to go to quarries and we used to use explosive to open up the magazines. You imagine enough explosive in there to blow a whole town up, and we used to blow it open. Explosive's very easy to handle. It's not dangerous. You can throw it on the fire. . . . I was like an apprentice. So we, my pal and I, decide to do our own safe-blowing. We managed to get hold of some explosives and our first job was on a safe—I can't tell you where because we've never been nicked for it—but we opened the safe as easy as that, and we had the money out, and that was the beginning of it. And then at various times we used to blow the store with explosives.

I remember once in Maidstone blowing a big magazine there, and I had two blokes with me, and they ran and kept running because when they found out I was going to blow the magazine open they thought I was crazy. But I opened it. Got the explosive out, but I noticed lots of white smoke used to come out and I'm sure that if there were any detonators there it would have blown the whole lot up—I know now—but the detonators were kept separate so you'd explode that one secondly, get the detonators out. We done it the hard way where you had to chisel your way into a magazine. It was very hard to get into—you could probably be there all night—where in a couple of minutes you could get it open and that's what we used to do and we done that on numerous occasions.

He acquired an intimate knowledge of explosives in the way that any crafts-man would with the tools of his craft. And the delight with which thirty years later he can still recite the rituals associated with his practice is testimony to the pride that he retains in his skill.

It's called Polo Ammond, and it was like mince-meat, red with all little red globules in it, and it was powerful enough to knock a door off a safe. The detonators were of a size that just used to fit into the keyhole of the safe, so you would take the baffle plate off the safe, load it up with enough explosive, put it all round in the lock, then you press your detonator in, run the wires off if it had wires, or if it had a fuse you just light the fuse and get out the way and the explosion occurs and you run back in. The door's usually laying on the floor. It was so easy. We were the scourge of London because we did all and sundry. I think I counted up when I was in jail and we did over 200 safes.

Dick Pooley was a consummate professional with a fierce streak of independ-ence, who saw no capital to be gained from aligning himself to an organization. However, he also acknowledges that without the co-operation of individuals with strategic knowledge of the market his craft becomes free-floating. This might lead to wasted time and resources, or even to reckless practice. Conse-quently the etiquette of the market was always adhered to and potentially valu-able intelligence was paid for.

We worked for ourselves mainly but the thief is only as good as the information that he can glean. If he can get good information, like the train-robbers. They were all petty criminals . . . I knew all of them, and they weren't all that bright, but they got information that there was money on that train and decided to do it and, you know, lots of people knew about it, but they did it. So they had good information so they had good money.

But we used to get people into us, that's why we blew so many safes. People would sidle up to us from the criminal fraternity and say 'Just seen it in the safe,' and we'd say to them 'How much?' 'Well, I dunno there's loads and loads of money going in, probably about a thick six inches or a foot, and they were piling it in the safe.' So we'd go and blow the safe open and probably find less than £100 or £200. And they were using our liberty really to get a few bob, because if we got good information we'd give them a third. There was two of us and if a bloke give us good information then he got a third. So people who knew this would take liberties really and do us up, so we used to do lots of safes and find nothing in them.

Dick Pooley is not only proud of his craft, but is also to this day explicit in his description of the narcissistic pleasure that he gained from competent practice. Yet his craft was not without its drawbacks, for apart from the obvious dangers implicit in explosive use, there were work-related maladies and injuries that still affect him three decades later.

Actually it used to get the old adrenaline running, and the two of us we loved what we did, and even today I never regret anything that I've done. And we had it all down to a fine art, and we done some nice things, and as I say we had too much bottle so other people, people that we were friendly with, wouldn't come out with us. They'd say 'You're crazy, the pair of you,' 'cos we would take chances, and I suppose we did take chances 'cos when you're in front of a safe putting explosives in, the sweat used to pour off you and there'd be a pool of water on the floor by the time you got the explosive in. It would run down your back, your legs, and drip on the floor—you were covered in sweat, and each time you blew that safe you would get nitro poisoning. You would get a terrible headache, and it was the daddy of all headaches, and apparently if you work in magazines where there is explosive, you're only supposed to work in them for twenty minutes. You must come out 'cos you get poisoned, and I was poisoned every time.

In the end it seemed that when the explosion occurred, then the head would come, and I'd be sick, and it seemed that the explosion set it off, so in the end I would load the safe, put my fingers in my ears, and then my partner who was the look-out man would leave his post as look-out, come back in, and he'd blow the safe so that I couldn't hear it. Every time I blew a safe I got nitro poisoning—it got through your fingers. I couldn't wear gloves 'cos I had to put the stuff in, and if you had gloves on, like tight rubber gloves, then it would restrict the blood, and your hands had to be loose so as you could get the stuff in quick and pack it nicely.

It used to do me up, the noise, and I can't stand noise now; noise really does me up, any sharp noise. In fact I'm going deaf. The doctor says 'Did you used to work amongst a lot of noise?' I said 'Yeah I used to open safes with explosives.' (Laughs). But you know, we done some nice and good things, and we lived well.

The decline of safe-cracking meant that Pooley, unlike the Silver Fox, had no one to pass his craft on to, yet in the demonology of British criminality as interpreted by the criminal justice system of the mid-1960s, a safe-cracker's pelt was highly prized.

[The police] hated us, and in fact I can always remember they never got nothing out of us. They beat us up, and beat us up badly, and in fact we—Alan Robinson, the Silver Fox, put us on to a job in Hampstead. We got into this place and I had a strange feeling.

The safe was there, we had the explosives, we were ready to blow the safe. It was on a main road but next door there was a pub, but I always get feelings—even today—I get feelings, and they turn out right. I said to Joe 'Joe, it's not right. There's something wrong here.' So all of a sudden we heard noises, and we got out the back, out the window, and went towards the gate. I landed up getting over the gate, Joe couldn't get over the gate. He was pulled back and sticks were . . . walloped him over the head, smashed his head, got him down—I'm away.

But they get into a car and they see where I'd hid in the front garden about half a mile away, and they come in and put the sticks on me. These two people were the two people who nicked the train-robbers, from Scotland Yard, and in evidence they said that they had been waiting in doorways across from the pub—we was only next door mind you—for Hindsy [Alfred Hinds, the notorious safe-cracker and prison escaper] had escaped and they were given information that he was going to be drinking in the pub, and so they were waiting to see if he went in the pub, but they heard us, which wasn't true, in the place next door. But we believe that we'd been set up and they were coming to nick us, which they did, and the Hindsy bit was a load of nonsense, and indeed Hindsy never showed up at that pub.

Judges too were keen on the demise of safe-cracking.

My last sentence, and I went out with another bloke who was a bit of a lunatic, and we landed up over in Lincoln blowing a safe belonging to the Geest banana company. And we opened the safe, blew it, and it just so happened that when we blew it a policeman walked by. So we had to leave the safe and the contents, all the money, and we got chased in our car. We had to abandon the car, and in the end we got caught and I landed up for blowing that safe in Lincoln in Spalding.

The Judge, a cunning man—landed up at the Old Bailey—terrible man, and I think a very dishonest man really, he was a vicious and cunning and evil man, one of the most evil judges; and it was a four-day trial, which was a trial within a trial. The barristers hated him. He used to come down to our cell—we were the only two in there—to check on the bolts to see we hadn't been sawing the bolts and bars to get out. I thought to myself, are we going to get a good crack of the whip with him? And then he said 'Never, never, in the history of' this little place. And you know the wind blows and rocks, and the wind was really pounding the place, rocking it about like, you know. 'Never has there been a more important case,' and he went on and on and on. What got us caught was a piece of paper.

When we were casing the job I went into a library and looked at a poetry book, and I come across a poem which I like to this day and it was by Christina G. Rossetti, so I wrote it down. 'Remember Christina G. Rossetti.' Well, when they found the car, this piece of paper was in the car, so the police spent weeks scouring London for a Miss Rossetti, but the judge pointed out to them during the summing-up, that although the police were looking for this woman, they weren't to know that she'd been dead for ninety years.

And at the end, before he sentenced me, he said 'I think there is no doubt in this court's mind that this man Pooley is one of the top safe-blowers in this country, and as such the public needs to be protected. But before I sentence him I think Pooley would appreciate this.' And he got a poetry book out and he read 'Remember me when I am gone away, gone far away . . .'. I can't remember it all but 'I can no more hold you by the hand'—this was a poem that she wrote about death, and he read it all out in the court to me, and my pal said to me 'Dick, we're going to get away with this.' I said 'Dave, this is the most cunning man I've ever been in front of, he's going to ten us up.' He said 'No, he's reading you a poem.' When he'd finished, then he came out and said 'You are known to the police to be one of the top safe-blowers in this country and as such the public needs to be protected. I sentence you to ten years in prison. TAKE HIM BELOW.' And he sentenced the other bloke to ten years' imprisonment—he fell down the stairs. (Laughs.) So we both got ten years for nothing really. So I decided to do me bird, come out, and turn it all in and to finish it.

Dick Pooley is in no doubt about the forces that connived in the decline of safe-cracking. The technological innovations that curtailed his practice are understood and clearly articulated. What shines through is the ego that informed his craft and manifests itself as an awesome self-belief.

Well, I think because of me they got better safes, and I knocked over 200 safes and they were so easy to knock over. They used to cement them down so you'd blow the door off. But if they weren't cemented down, twenty minutes you could have the back off. So Milner, who I could open their safes quite easy, joined up with Chatsworth Milner, and they now had a safe which was virtually blow-proof. In fact when you blew it, you blew it and it set off on springs a secondary mechanism so the bolts were shot home again. You'd made a lot of noise so you couldn't blow it again—you had to get out of there 'cos when the noise occurred you just had time to get your money and get off. . . . See, people graduated during my time from safes to banks, or to jugs as they'd call them. It was quicker to go and get it out with a shotgun, and they used to take all the money. That was the easy way, where doing it in the safe, you had to take a bit of time, lot of effort, lot of noise, and it took longer to do.

To understand the virtual extinction of Dick Pooley and his species, we must acknowledge the many parallels that their criminality had with the legitimate world of work in their era. They survived and prospered in a world of high times in low places, of craft apprentices learning at the lathe of semi-mythical masters, a world where the 'criminal fraternity' occupied a well-defined corner of post-war society that was rigidly stratified according to the individual's formally sanctioned occupational skills. Respect was paid to anyone with the skill to reap a successful living from a market-place that, compared to the maelstrom of modern criminality, was relatively calm. This enabled a continuity with the past and a belief in the future that carried with it echoes of shipyards, coal-mines, steel works, and other icons of proletarian identity that have since joined Britain's industrial museum.

But all of us, I think, we were all born too late, 'cos I think if we'd been born 200 year ago we'd have all been pirates, all earning plenty of money and getting gold and all the rest of it. . . . You open a safe and you think this is the one. And you open another one and this has got to be the one. It's like the gold prospector, he keeps digging and digging until he finds. And you find that a lot of criminals are very persistent people, they keep at it, sometimes until the day they die and never realize, but some do, but they keep trying.

THE THIEF

What I always like about these things like on the box when they say 'I got in with a bad crowd and they just led me on, Your Honour.' That just don't stand up, 'cos I was in with a good crowd, good meaning, good earners, always got plenty of money. So when I get the chance I don't go in the factory knocking my pipe out for a two-bob job; I'm going ducking and diving with the people who know what the game is. When it came to working I was learning how to make money from nothing, and you don't get that from the ordinary people, so you find them who are like you, and just find that the others who are at it are the only ones who know.

Robin's school years were spent in a succession of foster homes and orphanages, before he graduated to the crime academies that dominated the penal landscape of the late 1950s.

My old man was in the Navy and something occurred between him and me mum, so I was shunted around these places until somebody come for me, some auntie and uncle. Then when that never worked out it was back to some place in the country. I would go out for the others, thieving for food, 'cos there was never enough, and it was shitty, if you don't mind me saying so. Sloppy food, and kids fighting and crying, and the staff was like army people, shouting and banging about. I was in this place in Suffolk, and one of the workers was a prisoner of war with the Japanese. He was all right most of the time, but when he had to sleep in at night he used to cry all the time, all night just crying and crying. If you got caught thieving like from the kitchen, they just beat you up in front of the others with everybody watching.

When we was out somewhere I just thieved anything—clothes, money, food whatever there was, I just took it without thinking. 'Cos we had nothing, you see—we wasn't allowed nothing, so if we went to the seaside for the day I would hoover it up, whatever was going. I wasn't the only one. You get these little kids from somewhere, didn't know where they were, and you just go 'Do this, take that', and there you go, they all wanted to be one of the boys, and if you got caught, well, we was getting beaten up anyway so it never made much difference. It was the same whether you was talking in class, or breaking into the kitchens, so you just got used to it.

Eventually Robin left school and worked initially as an apprentice to a firm of french polishers, but this did not prove to be particularly lucrative, and after a few months he left to begin a succession of manual jobs while developing some expertise as a burglar.

There was this market—gone now, but it was the kind that had these lock-ups, and night time there was nobody about, so you could do the lock-up in a bit of peace. That's when I started doing motors to shift the stuff. I would do toys, anything really, but cloth and material was favourite. In the motor and away to this bedsit place I stayed at. The

landlady there, she would buy all I had. Had a shed at the back and just put it in there.
She was like dealing with all the other market people knocking out this gear, and that's
how it came on top. The market people was buying their own gear back and I got nicked.

I got every market lock-up put down to me, and it was two years in ———. When I was
there there was this PTI knew my old man from the Navy. He used to slip me a packet
of fags, and it was all right really, just like the homes I was in—just more of the same.
As long as you could look after yourself, you just rode it out and the food was all right.

Robin went through three custodial sentences before he had reached 25, when,
as the father of two girls, he felt obliged to make some substantive provision for
their future. Up to that point he had been an all-purpose thief with a penchant
for warehouses and no record of violence. His involvement in armed robbery
was simply the result of his desire to make a lot of money as quickly as possible.
There was no ideological shift, and culturally there was no occupational hier-
archy to negotiate. Robin was greedy, and willing to make the leap from simple
theft to violence, yet certainly in retrospect he can acknowledge the raising of
the stakes that this involved. Even if Robin can rationalize his activities in terms
of the similarities between simple theft and armed robbery, particularly in terms
of the fundamental qualities that are required, he recognizes that society will
inevitably focus upon the enabling methodologies rather than follow the money.

Whatever you got you want more—that's the way we all are. It's like anything else. You
start off with something, and it seems like enough. But really it's family. When you got
kids around you, you start worrying if they will be all right, and if the bills will get paid
if you go away. The money don't go as far as it used to, and you start to feel like you
should be stretching out now for more. . . . You want better things—motors and a proper
home, if you got kids. The other thing is that you know if you go blagging, then nobody
is going to be earning more, and all the dodging about when you are just thieving and
buying and selling for a couple of grand, you know, in a few minutes you can earn a few
years' worth of all that, so that was for me. . . . The risk is there, but the money was more
to the point.

Robin allied himself with two men who had reputations for violence, and
along with a succession of drivers robbed a number of banks and building
societies.

Until I started I never knew a thing about shooters. We never spent more than a few days
sussing out where we was going to do some work. They knew I was for money, and we
would sort it out about a week beforehand and just take the prize.

Although up to this point Robin had not attempted to use violence as a money-
making device, and there is nothing to suggest that he possessed anything approaching a violent reputation, he had been well schooled in the potential of
violence.

Let me put it this way, if you had stitched me up in a deal, I would have come round
and done what was the right thing to get the money you owed me. If you don't do that,

then you get put down as a self-caterer—a wanker—and then everybody lines up to take your money. So it's just a case of being able to look after yourself, and I was known as somebody who could do that.

The working arrangements were almost casual, with little planning and a cavalier regard for detail.

I just used to get a sawn-off given to me by one of the others and go to work. In the door and either hold the floor so it was nice and calm, or over the top for the money. I never even noticed the others in there—I just did the job and got out.

Even when it came on top what I did I just heard it all and never even reacted. I was getting on with my little number, and these guards were in the jug picking up money, and we never even knew they was there until we got inside. We never noticed the van or nothing. They started running about round these people we had on the floor, and I never really took it in. Then like in slow motion one of these is running almost past me like I'm not there, so I give this one with the helmet a whack, but he kept coming, so I pointed it at him and started screaming, and he got down on the floor with the others. My pal, who was on the other side, let go with the sawn-off, and one of the others who was holding a money-bag, he was hit. The noise, I can hear it now. We still got the prize though.

The weapons were found in the garden shed of a relation of one of the villains, and Robin was convicted and sentenced to fourteen years.

I was a steady worker and it did feel good to be respected like that. You can't panic, and people respect you if you just do a good job and don't let anybody down. That goes for the people you rob too. . . . They want to feel that you are in control of everything, so that they don't feel that they have got to have a pop. They just want to lie there till it's over, and the quicker the better. The better you are at the job, the better they like it.

This is the key to defining the robber's competence: obtaining sufficient levels of compliance from workers and members of the public to enable the efficient extraction of large quantities of cash. However, not all robbers possess sufficient levels of competence to ensure that the operation will progress according to plan.

Our little firm did all right, but we never took it all that seriously. . . . I knew a little firm that were doing what two, three betting-shops a fortnight, and they are all—what twenty years later—more—all wealthy men with a lot of prime property. By the time I come out, nobody was doing what we was doing, not regular. It was changing, and where you used to go to the Artists and some of the other places 'cos it was the place to be, and everybody else who was at it would float in for a drink, no more—it was different. . . . The people was the same, well some of them, some of them was away, but they was doing a different kind of thing—more straight but, well, business, I suppose. They was iffy business people now, instead of just iffy. (Laughs.) . . . Property and things to do with property was what was the thing.

However, Robin was in no position to join in the 1970s property boom. The money had evaporated over the years, and an attempt at reconciliation with his family proved unsuccessful. Soon he was offered employment at his old trade and within three years had acquired a jewellery business, a new wife, and a suburban home.

This time we knew what we were doing a lot more, and we took it serious. . . . no fucking about laughing and that. I mean when we were at it before, we are going in just in the car ready, and my pal says 'Right, I'm tooled up.' So we all look, 'cos we are all tooled up, I mean proper, but he's got a fucking catapult in his hand going 'Anybody fucks about with me and they are going down.' (Laughs.)

This time we were more careful about things and we made money. We took our time about a target and we were making money and being careful. There was hardly any heavy involved, and I was living away from it all. It was lorries, warehouses, anything where there was a real result.

Then when I was nicked the last time, they did the full bit with the early raid and the door gets put in. By now I was known and it was a matter of time anyway, but I can honestly hold my hand up and say I was stitched up totally. They marked an A to Z that was in my motor on the page where there was a blag. Then they rowed in a shooter that they found at —— house, and lumped it all in one, and I topped up six years. . . . I mean, well at it, and that we all were—plenty of money and we put some aside. We knew what it was about, but we were never done for the work that we did over that time, so it sticks in the throat a bit.

That was it for me. That world is gone. The people are different. Some are still about, but this business is what I got out of it, and, not that I am the Pope or nothing, but it comes down to really being at it, I mean at the heavy and that. Well, those days are over, we all know that. . . . I am too old to be charging about. I mean, you still play football? I mean, when you ask me about being criminal, it's not the nerve has gone, but the nerve changes. You get more interested in what to do with the dough, how to move it about and work it. That's more important than how you get it, somehow.

Robin had always been a thief. From his earliest exploits as a burglar to his brief but profitable career as an armed robber, the master status of thief is not something that he shies away from.

If you say to me what am I, what do I do, I got to say to you that I am a thief. That's what I do. I see what people got, take it, and sell it. Just like I say to you 'What are you?' You going to tell truth, you say I'm a teacher or whatever. Now some people, they say 'I got a business' or 'I don't work', then you see them out wheeling and dealing, at it with big wodges of notes. But me, I'm up front, I am a thief and I do a little bit of the other thing, but really what I am is a thief.

We all change as we get older, but really we are the same. I am still a thief. . . . All right, in a different way, but it's to do with thieving, sort of low key; you might call it receiving. I move stuff for other people, but, well, one of the things I wanted to say was, it depends what you mean when you talk about criminals and that. I mean, look at that (points to menu): 'Fruits of the Forest', what's that? What fruit, when was anybody here in a forest? It's a con. Look at that (sign). It says 'Exit', but that's the kitchen. . . . Pictures look: there's no cars—no cars—and when did the Queen look like that? Everybody is at it. These people are, and it's a big chain. They're lying all the time. But there's not that little edge that you might get captured. And that's the difference.

My daughter fitted her kitchen, and the dope what did it couldn't saw wood, but the money he was charging was proper fitter prices. That's criminal—he is at it. He is a criminal. But he don't in any shape or form think that he is, but I (*sotto voce*) fucking do. If I do something a bit slippery and it comes on top, I can't say 'I'm no good, that's all—you can't nick me.' But this little fucker, he's billing me £250 a day, and I'm supposed to keep a straight face. He was useless, believe me. . . . Is that criminal? Is that taking money out of people's pocket? 'Course it is. Nobody's put a gun to your head, but you are just as done, just as well fucking skint when he's gone, 'cos he's got what's yours.

Unless you are the village idiot with nothing, then somebody's doing damage to you, but they won't have Bill banging on their door at five o'clock tooled up with marked notes for the fridge. Do you see me? Anybody now can make a lot of money without all that. But it's all one and the same. . . . It's all one, and for some of it you get nicked, for some of it you get a slap. Criminal's not in it. All anybody does, anybody, is take the money and do a runner.

Robin is now a dinosaur. Specialist blaggers are few and far between, and as guns are easier to get, reckless amateurs are targeting shops, garages, and off-licences for derisory sums of money. But we now live in a society dominated by the language and ethics of business, rather than the Wild West, and even robbers like Robin eventually acquire a legitimate business interest as a suitably ironic finale to their career. Far better to be business-like from day one, to supply commodities to those that demand them, to work in an industry that uses violence as an instrument of commercial control rather than as a primary means of capital acquisition.

There is little scope for irony in the repertoire of young business people of the 1990s. Since childhood they have been enveloped in the once-fashionable creed of enterprise. They embrace profit rather than the macho blag-speak of the balaclava and sawn-off shotgun brigade. Their enterprise is demand-led, and the customer is always right. Moira is about as far away from the drug-pushing demon of the tabloid headlines as could be imagined. In her late twenties, expensively dressed, and with poise beyond her years, she would not look out of place behind the scenes of a merchant bank, or City finance house. Moira is a commodity broker.

THE DEALER

Moira's entrance into crime was based upon the rational acknowledgement that an entrepreneurial opportunity was staring her in the face. The chance of making money from crime was made apparent to her by the evident incompetence of her boyfriend. She sells dope.

I was going out with someone who was in the same line of business, which is quite common believe it or not. A lot of people who are in that line of business, they also take in the merchandise as it were, so that doesn't exactly help for a clear head, but unless you can calculate how much you're going to come out with at the end and so on, it's no good. So a lot of the times he'd end up doing stuff that in fact wouldn't really be worth it, and that's how I got a lot of the contacts through that. That's how it started. I'd do the money side of it, and I'd do all the calculations, because if you're in a situation when you're setting something up, people upping and downing the price, and you'd be trying to knock things off so . . . I'd go and do the money side of it, count it up and down, or hold the money and stuff like that. I used to do kilos of dope, which is what I still do.

I mean coke makes a lot more money and most people do that these days, most people do that for better return, as the saying goes, but I prefer to do just straightforward dope, I find that it's just a bit safer. The return isn't as good but I feel a bit happier with it. . . . Coke, people are addicted to coke, so you're more likely to have trouble with other people because it's like a much heavier drug to be dealing with than it is with dope.

The humdrum nature of her everyday routine is, as Moira recognizes, in stark contrast to popular images of drug-dealing. She operates in a world that is some way removed from both inner-city sleaze and jet-set glamour. She despises her customers and has managed to identify mutual distrust as the pivotal instinct upon which her enterprise thrives.

Well, a lot of it's just waiting around and you spend a lot of time of the phone. Most people have got a mobile these days. It's not safe to do it on your own phone. What would happen, you'd be chatting with people on the phone, ringing up your contacts . . . it's like you're just on the phone the whole time, just finding out what's occurring, who's wanting what. People are ringing you up saying 'I want this, I want that'. Then you'll be ringing other people to see what's around, or you might know that something's going to be happening in a week's time and you've got an order in for that, and then it's like keeping ringing up, finding out what's happening. . . . and then you've got to have your money ready, to go and sort it out.

There are few clues to the essential criminality of Moira's business. The commercial intricacies of the enterprise are not couched in a complex code that alludes to dark, seductive alcoves of villainy. Such elaborations are increasingly the province of arcane boys' games.

Well it is a business—it's like any sort of business. There is a certain way of doing things really, and you do have to know the way of doing things. The other thing about dope is that a lot of people who do dope have a set lot of customers who'll always buy from them, and that's what they'll do. I know people I sell to, they've got a set lot of people who'll they'll maybe give out 5 ounces, 6 ounces, whatever, to them, and they have almost like a set order with people because a lot of people smoke dope. I don't think people realize how many people smoke regularly, continually, and always have to have a supply, because it is definitely a most common thing.

You have people come round for it, and that's why I'd never have people come round—now that is boring and that is a real pain. You have people come round your house all the time to buy stuff, and then you have to be nice to them, and they come round and they end up staying in your living-room, and you've got to have a smoke with them. I'm not saying this is the case with everybody, but it's boring. You know, it's your house and you've got people coming to your house and hanging out in your lounge and they think it's really cool or whatever . . . It's not at all glamorous; in fact it's really boring, it is really boring. It's like a boring thing. It's a lot of waste of time, and you have to deal with a lot of dickheads all the time. . . . There's some really all right people, and I've got good friends, but my actual friends are not people I do business with, because it's no good. It's absolutely no good, because it's too heavy, because a lot of the time you are ripping people off, because that's what it's all about in a lot of ways, and people will try and get one over on you, and you've got to try and protect yourself against that.

There's no sort of good business sense about it. The whole idea is it's a dodgy business—if somebody can rip you off they will do. How will they rip you off? Selling you under, selling you shit, giving you a taste of something then selling you something different, taking money and not coming up with the goods. There's loads of ways of that happening to you. The other thing that can happen is you go to a meet and you've got money, and then they haven't got the goods and you get your money nicked, and that's happened to me. But most of the time you're dealing with people you know, and it's today an advantage not to do that to you because they've got to move their stuff, and you're another link in the chain, and particularly if they've got to get rid of it quick, it can't happen. Especially when I was moving about 4 kilos a week, which is not a lot really. . . .

If you sell short weight that's the traditional way of doing it. You can mix them up. There's ways you can make hash go further. It's fucking hard work. It's not worth the bother I think, but people do it. Or you could sell just slightly short—that's why you should always take your own scales . . . but again that's a dangerous thing to do because if you're walking the streets with a pair of electric scales it's kind of hard to explain what you've got them for really.

Moira uses her gender in the course of her business every bit as blatantly, and probably more efficiently, than most armed robbers. She is aware of the assumptions that most men will make about a woman's business acumen and negotiating skills, and regards these assumptions as a weakness which, along with her appearance, she is prepared to exploit.

I get away with a lot more in terms of not having any sort of police attention because the way I look, the way I dress, the way I carry on my life is not the sort of way that anybody would think that was particularly dodgy. The fact that I've got a mobile phone is, I think, particularly dodgy, but I mean other people have mobile phones, electricians, so anybody who has a mobile phone doesn't mean they're dodgy, but on the other hand . . . No, it is an issue because they're . . . well, for a start they (men) think they can get one over on you, which is an advantage in a way, because they do treat me like I'm a bit dumb occasionally, which is quite funny because I'm not, but that's quite a laugh because they do underestimate my intelligence at times. 'Cos they think they're dead smart about the money, they can cut up the money, but in fact I can cut it up a lot quicker, and that's when I manage to get one over on people, because they think that they're pulling a fast one, and in fact I end up turning it round the other way and saying 'OK, well I'll have this for that and this for that'. And it ends up actually I'll have made, knocked a oner off the deal, and still getting the same money, and it's only when they've agreed to it and they'll go 'Oh, hang on a sec', and of course they've agreed to it and you just say 'Oh well, blah, blah', and get the money out. Getting the money out usually settles the deal.

But there are some practical disadvantages to being a woman in the drug trade, which make it difficult for Moira to exclude men from her enterprise completely.

I have a partner who is a man. You have to do—you can't deal on your own as a woman. . . . It's not safe. You have to have somebody with you. You could get ripped off, and it's just not safe. You have to have a bloke, and often you have to have somebody to front it for you, because it might be your money. . . . Certainly, people get to know that you've got maybe money, or gear, at your house and you're practically likely to get held up or robbed, or taxed, as they say. If you're quite good-looking you can appeal to various people's whatever, and get away with stuff like that. Just like being really nice and looking nice gets their guard down a bit.

I said 'And then you rip them off—do a good deal.'

Do a good deal, I think. It's the whole idea of the business. It's up to you to protect yourself from a dodgy deal. It's up to you, and if you can't protect yourself from that, well then you're a mug and that's your problem, it's not anybody else's problem and that's the way it runs. You know if you're a mug you'll get stitched up and that's your problem. That's the way it is. So in a way that's good, that makes people favour and it appeals to them, it's a bit more glamorous for them. It's not a glamorous business, it's a horrible . . . it's not at all glamorous, there's nothing glamorous about it, nothing goes on in posh hotels, nobody meets under clocks in stations, there's nothing like James Bond, nothing glamorous about it at all. Maybe if you get into top level it is glamorous because you've got a lot more money, but it's not glamorous, so maybe dealing with a woman is a bit more glamorous, I don't know.

Even her dealings with the police involve the manipulation of male gender expectations.

Well, yeah, I have had a couple of near misses. The worst one was when I got stopped in the car and I had actually got somebody with me who had a lot of form, and they were going 'Is this your new bird?' and everything, and he's going . . . 'cos he's such a fucking arsehole . . . he's going 'Oh yeah, yeah', and I'm going 'Oh, for Ch——. Oh, please.' They've asked me what my name is and I've given them a name and they're checking through the car and of course I've got some stuff in the car. Normally I wouldn't have somebody around, but it was a contact and we were going to somebody else's friend so we're going in the car.

Moira had 4 kilos of dope in the boot of her car.

Anyway, we're in the car and they're giving him a load of hassle and making him take everything out of his pockets and everything like that, and I was thinking 'Oh fuck, they're going to start looking in the back of the car', but it was my car and so they were trying to ask me how I knew him and everything, and the stupid bastard said I was his girlfriend, and I'm going 'He's lying—I'm not his girlfriend. I've just been out on a date with him a couple of times.' They're going 'Do you know who he is?' and I said 'Oh no, I just met him in a pub.' They're giving me all this and I start doing all the really Miss Innocent . . . fortunately I look quite smart, so I started doing Miss Innocent, and this sort of fatherly copper said 'You do realize who he is, don't you?' and I'm going like 'No, no, has he been in trouble then?' and he's going 'Oh yeah, he's got form as long as your arm,' and I'm going 'Oh God, my mum will kill me.' I'm practically crying, you know, and I turned round to him and goes 'You're not getting back in my car. They've just told me that you're a big nerd.' And he's going 'What, you what' and I'm going 'You told me in the pub that you were in business,' and getting really hysterical. So of course they don't want to have a hysterical woman, so they're going 'All right, love, all right.' So I'm going 'Can I go now, can I go now?' So they said 'Oh yeah, of course you can.' So I just get in the car again and drive off. I was just sweating so much because I've really had to put out this guy, and he's left standing on the pavement. So that's a funny story. So the coppers who stopped us on that day—this poor distressed Northerner. Suckers. (Laughs.)

I asked her why she was getting out of the business.

Because I think there's a limit to how long you can carry on really. Because you get the money side of it, I'm not saying I make a lot of money but I do make good money. You know, it's not worth you doing it if you don't make a reasonable amount of money. . . . I mean, I know a lot of people who've got away with it for years. I know quite a lot more people who haven't, and in a way the longer you carry on the more likely you are to get nicked really. It only takes somebody to open their mouths to the wrong person and, you know. I think there is a certain amount of controlled dealing about the place . . . anyway, I mean, I know people who have been nicked . . . see I've never been nicked, you see, so I think for people who have been nicked there is a certain sort of, not a relationship going on. The police know them and they maybe keep an eye on them from time to time, because it's a way of them finding out what's actually happening. I will miss the money side of it. I always have a draw, always having a draw, I think that's what I'm going to miss, but I don't think that's going to be a problem, to be honest. I think the only other thing I might miss a little bit is the fact that you have got a lot of flexibility. One of the things I did do was stash up money and go away.

But I've done a lot now. It's like you don't know—you see people who've been doing it for years and years and years and that's their way of life and I just think, well, maybe it's time to have a bit of change. I've always tried to keep a bit of legitimate something on the side, because you do need to have a way of explaining things, because . . . well, I don't really exist in a way. What's been the hardest thing for me is explaining to people what I'm actually doing, and of course when you start doing that, then it becomes harder, because of lots of other people like, as you say, like tax. Trying to explain to the tax where you've been for six or seven years is kind of difficult, and there's only so much travelling you can blag. I know people who've done exactly that. They've made their money and got a shop or a business, and that's what they do now, and they make good money.

Moira is sensitive to changes in the market, noting the arrival of new commodities and the revival of old favourites. Yet her sensitivity to the whims of the market-place does not override her remarkably ethical concerns with the impact of increased chemical consumption upon young people.

There's a lot more coke for a start-off. . . . Ecstasy and acid, LSD . . . Es and trips have meant now that people who wouldn't have taken drugs, who would have probably just gone down the pub, are taking drugs now, and they have to get them from somewhere, so they're going to get into contact with somebody who's selling. So I think that's really changed since I was a teenager, that has changed. When I was a teenager we used to take speed, but it wasn't as common as Es are now. When I go out now, it's like 16- and 18-year-olds absolutely off their faces.

But the bottom line is business, and the customer is always right.

I think they're both [ecstasy and LSD] very powerful drugs. I know that might sound a bit moralistic, but they're both powerful drugs. I went out a load in 1988–9, and still do go out and get off my head, but I think if I'd have done that to the degree and as often and as bang on, as full on as some of these people are doing at that age, I think I would have totally fried my brains, and I think it's much harder to handle at that age. I mean it's just really a very emotional experience, and I know I might sound a bit like an old hippie, but you've got to take these things seriously.

In the sixties and even the seventies trips were like, you'd take a trip and you'd stay in because it was too powerful to go out . . . You wouldn't go out dancing all over the place—it was great. I think tripping was slightly safer, but on the other hand it's not really—its a powerful thing, it's a powerful drug, and I think we haven't really thought what's going to happen to everybody. But then again in the sixties, they say the sixties was bad for drugs, but it wasn't—most people didn't come across drugs at all, from what I've heard. But on the other hand you've got to do everything from a business point of view. If people are doing Es and trips they all want smoke to come down, which is great, thank you.

Craftsmen are redundant, artisans devalued; it is the entrepreneur who thrives. Parallels with the legitimate world are irresistible. The market, rather than some cosy, familiar macho world of hard men and cheeky chappies, now dominates. If the unwritten code of the underworld ever existed, it is now as outdated as an Ealing comedy. As this chapter has progressed, the jokes have become fewer and farther between. The articulated warmth has faded, and the rationale has become more stark. Moira sees crime for what it is—a means of making money. She sees no need for it to be anything else. No adrenaline, no camaraderie, no craft. Just buyers and sellers.

2

Man and Boy: The Violence of Enterprise

After I got my first few bucks and the nerve to go shopping without my mother, I went to Benny Field's on Pitkin Avenue. That's where the wiseguys bought their clothes. I came out wearing a dark-blue pin-striped, double-breasted suit with lapels so sharp you could get arrested for just flashing them. I was a kid, I was so proud. When I got home my mother took one look at me and screamed, 'You look just like a gangster!' I felt even better.

(N. Pileggi, *Wise Guy*)

It would be unwise to attempt to comprehend the lives of Danny, Chris, and Jimmy, without first assembling the intricate web of relationships between their identities and the structures that underpin their day-to-day existence. Crime for these three men is a tool they use to carve a slice of life's loot. That their personal identities were obviously forged within family units that were explicitly patriarchal is self-evident. The economic base and subsequent strategies developed by the two families are qualitatively different, but both are situated around a cultural frame of tough, resourceful masculinity that transcends both economic epochs and generational responses to communal problems. Violence can function as a bridge between personal and economic universes, between the worlds of family and work, men and women, father and son. It is an enduring, emphatically masculine resource that is not only inherited but also licensed by the family and all the other agencies that are part of the informal order of the market-place.

Violence is an integral theme of the childhoods of these three men and has played an essential part in forming their adult identities. Their reputation as men of violence enables them to occupy a space between the market-place and a moral vacuum that exists beyond stock clichés of utilitarianism and instrumentality.[1] Indeed they are as likely to resort to violence over a business dispute as they are over a game of darts, a slander against their local football team, or a hard look in a mean pub from a dangerous stranger.

Danny is 44 years old, about 5 foot 7, and 15 stone, balding, with tattoos on both forearms, a scar under his left eye, and multiple indentations on his forehead. Chris is 23 years old, also about 5 foot 7, and 14 stone, with a rapidly receding hairline, a crescent-shaped scar on his chin, and a woman's name tattooed on his left forearm. They are father and son.

An earlier version of this chapter appeared in T. Newburn and B. Stanko (eds.), *Just Boys Doing Business* (London: Routledge, 1995).

DANNY. He is like me and he knows it—plays on it since he was a babe. Copied everything. When I had the fucking hump so did he! So I come in, got the fucking hump with Sheila, then he turns round, little kid I'm talking about here, he throws his dinner up the wall and bowls out. Then he starts coming out with me—I'm doing a little deal, like a delivery or that—and it's all 'Look at him. Chip off the old block. Don't he look like his dad.' You know, play with him, sweets, fucking cakes, the lot. He walks like me—always has . . . and I showed him things, told him don't take liberties, but don't take any shit. You gotta be first—if there's gonna be a ruck, just go straight in, steam in and fucking hurt them . . . I used to train him up, put a bag up, old kitbag full of rags, and teach him how to punch. Could punch and all, always had a dig on him . . . I got him one of those punch-balls that you stand on and a pair of gloves, sparring with him, hands up, elbows in.

CHRIS. Loved it, going out with the old man in the van. He had a lorry too—big Volvo unit. The best was a long run out Southampton or Tilbury to pick up a trailer. We'd stop off at cafés, big breakfasts. He knew all the people, the drivers and the people who ran the places . . . It was great, like when all the others was at school I was out in a unit and seeing all the countryside. The punch-ball, Christmas present, red plastic thing with like a stand you stand on to keep it up. I'd box with him, he would go down on his knees and spar around. If I fucked it up, he'd give me a slap. Never really let me give him a good slap and that's all I wanted to do—hit him. I am like him, I look like the old photos, but he was so over the top it wasn't true.

Once I was outside playing, kicking a ball about or something, after school, and he pulls up in the van, runs in the house, comes out with a handful of knives. Mum tried to stop him, gets in the van, and drives off fast like. Then one of me mates says that your dad's been in a fight. I was having me tea and a knock on the door. This bloke near us says to Mum that Dad's been stabbed, he's in hospital. He come home next morning, stitches in his arm and a lump on his head. That was the end of it. But he could be evil; he was always having a ruck. When we moved there was all this stuff on the pavement, boxes and that. He reckoned that somebody had his records. This is the first day we got there. So he's gone next door with this long screwdriver, put their windows out. Always rucking.

DANNY. There was no peace. I'd come home, had the lorry and that, and sometimes I'd be gone two to three days wheeling, dealing, earning, and then I'd come home and the fucking noise: he's done this, she's done that. I'd sit there with a cup of tea and the noise would just build up, you know what kids are like, and I just want some peace.

Sooner or later I'd just blow. I'd whack Chris—not whack, just slap 'im, tell 'er to fucking button it, get a bath, and go and have a drink. I wasn't violent. He says I was—I fucking wasn't. Now you know me, if I want to have a ruck I will have one. I was gonna be violent, I'd kill him. But it wasn't like that . . . I just wanted some quiet and it would start I'd tell him to shut up and he would give me some lip. Always up front he has been. I'd say did you do that and he'd say 'Yeah, so what.' I'd give him a dig and he'd say 'One day I'll be bigger than you and I'll beat you up.' Fucker is big now and strong. I mean if I can lift 200 lbs, then he can do 250. But I tell him, don't mess about with me, boy, I'm in my prime. (Laughs.)

CHRIS. I know I fucking hated him. He'd give me a slap, then just stand there and look at me. Put me across the fucking room sometimes, then stand there giving it the big un. So when I was about 14 I thought, that's it, so I hit him hard—punched him in the face. Shouted 'I'm a man now' or something fucking stupid. He walked out the house—just went don't know where, just went. I went to bed shitting myself. Next morning he never come back. That night he comes in like nothing was on, just normal like, sits down. Then when I was having my tea he just punches me in the head. I thought he was going to kill me. I was on the floor and he's hitting me with a chair. Mum got him off. He was saying 'Wanna be a man, I'll treat you like a man.'

DANNY. I remember I walked out 'cos I would have killed him. Stayed out, away, just didn't want to know. But inside I was boiling. I can't stand anybody raising their hands to me. It was tea-time and I just went . . . That's it really. Tom and fucking Jerry, that's us. Always a war going on.

CHRIS. What do you do? You want to be one of the boys, so you do all the usual stuff, running with hounds, getting in bits of shit here and there. You start feeling your way and, all right, I was a bit lippy, but there was no room at home and we started getting in each other's way. I didn't like being hit by him all the time. He'd come in when he had a drink, and Mum would start saying he's done this and that. I never hung about—went out the back way over the wall. Caught me once, threw a dustbin at me, full fucking bin, hit me in the back up the wall. I scratched his car—never told him that. (Laughs.) Went right outside and scratched his car.

At 13 Chris joined the pool team of the local pub, and Danny took a great deal of pride in his son's skill. Pool was important to Danny for a number of reasons. It was a sport that he could play when 4 or 5 stone overweight, and there was a great deal of status to be derived from being a good pool-player. Most importantly, pool-playing creates and demands a most specific economy of movement and style, an aggressive yet quite subtle catalogue of stalking, and striking poses that are designed for maximum drama, derived essentially from masculine urban street style.

CHRIS. I was good—fast. Quick weren't in it. I could play. They used to see this little kid and be all nice, you know. 'There, there sonny.' . . . Then I clear the table and they go, well, quiet, I suppose.

DANNY. He was so out of order. Good, very good—he learnt quick. I used to take him in the pub and he would play the machines, game of darts, whatever. Then they got the table and he was at it all the time, all his money went in it. Sometimes he would just stand like a little puppy-dog with a cue in his hand waiting for some poor wanker to pity him and give him a game. But as he got better he got fucking murder; he started winding people up. Like they'd miss a pot or something and he'd scream 'Oh, unlucky,' top of his voice. Wind people up terrible. I had a word in his ear lots of times. 'Don't wind people up. You gonna get a slap off someone soon.' Trouble was when he was playing for the pub he's got everybody shouting 'Go on Chrissie, do 'im,' and laughing when he fucks about.

CHRIS. I was a mouthy fouler, but I loved it . . . The old man, all the pub in there, watching. I just showed out, just put on a show. Then we got barred. It wasn't me, well it was a bit, but the old man, he just blew, and that was it.

DANNY. We had a match against the 'Carpenters'. We know them all, don't we? I mean, they are just round the corner. Most of them drink in the Bulldog anyway. They all knew Chrissie from a kid, but he still takes the piss, on and on. In the end Peter comes up, their captain like, and just asks me to calm him down. If it stayed like that, then it would have blew over, but right after, one of theirs comes over and says something about whacking him, and don't care if he is a kid. So I captures [Chris], pulls him outside, and gives him the fucking news. Tells him 'Stop taking the piss.' I slaps him about a bit, let him know I fucking mean it, then goes back inside. Dick, I stewed on it. We are into afters now. The match is finished, but he was there, the one who said he would give Chrissie a whack, and I went and just did him.

Danny hit the man several times with a heavy ashtray before he was pulled off. However, in extricating Danny from the maul a female supporter of the opposing team had her handbag trodden on, which in turn led to punches being thrown by her companion, an elderly man who had recently suffered a stroke. When he was knocked to the floor, the intensity of the fracas escalated and bottles and pool cues were wielded. The fight, which involved over twenty men and women, spilled out into the street and both Danny and Chris were slightly injured.

DANNY. Old Bill turns up and it stopped like it does. The geezer I whacked was still out, and when they were seeing to him Chrissie and most of the others pisses off. I got pulled along with my mate Billy, but it comes to fuck all. I get out next morning, usual thing, very polite, Sign here sir, no charges, have a nice fucking day and piss off.'
CHRIS. When he came back he knocked the shit out of me. Why? I suppose as I was getting too leery like. It was nothing, just a ruck, just another ruck, but he could have a ruck, the old man.

Danny was sent to a special school at the age of 12 after his widowed mother remarried.

DANNY. My old man was without a doubt a diamond. Everybody knew him. We used to go out totting and I would go with him. Had this old horse at the back of the prefabs pulling a cart, and I would trot along the street, knocking on the doors while Dad would shout and sing. Yeah, sing, like opera. (Sings.) 'Have you got any rag and bone or mangles, woollens or cottons, I give you best prices.' He boxed as well, in the Army . . . all England knew him. Died when I was 9 or 10, I think. He was only about 40, not that probably, nearer 35.
When Mum got married it didn't seem right. See, Dad never hit me. He would have a row with anybody like anybody, but he wasn't what you would call a hard man. He was a singer. On a Sunday morning he would do the breakfast and I would lay in bed waiting, and he would just make up these songs. I dunno . . . (Sings.) 'Get out of bed and getta your double egg, bacon, bubble and two fried slices.' He was a good old boy, my Dad. Like I said, when Mum got married again he would try to make me do things, but I just used to go missing. I'd sleep the night in the old buildings. There was an old Anderson shelter at the back of the match factory and that was that. I didn't want to know. Tops up got sent to this school out in the country near——. Loved it—nobody hit nobody else. The teachers, they were your friends. I had girlfriends, played guitar, sort of place you don't want to leave. But you do, like, when you leave school, and that was it.—— [his stepfather] got me a job as a van boy. I never minded it really. Got enough to get by. But it meant living at home, so I just got out when I could.

Danny became part of a slightly older group which frequented an illegal drinking club in Stepney.

DANNY. I was just sort of around the edge, 'cos I was a few years younger than the others. Money was easy, like they would always buy. And this will shock you, I wasn't a drinker, a light ale or two, then just coffee. The others was well into drink, but they earnt well, all of them. Market porters some of 'em, lorry-drivers, plenty of money. And they was all at it, anything, buying, selling.

There was an old geezer in the —— [a club]. We thought he owned it, but he never. He would always buy a piece of tom [jewellery] or a watch, and some of the boys, they would do a deal with him over a ring or whatever. One night there was this geezer, brother of one of the others, been going on about how his firm had a room at the back with gear in it—fuck knows what it was, can't remember. Anyway, we went in, got nothing out of it, but we was off then. God's truth, up to then nothing, I was not interested, never done a thing. Then after that happened I was well at it, good an' all.

Danny changed jobs many times between the ages of 15 and 17, and criminal activity took up an increasing amount of his social and working life.

DANNY. I was a grafter, I loved to graft . . . Over a wall, back of a lorry, didn't matter, and work too—I just chased money. I did van jobs, buildings, anything. Had a pop at scaffolding. Fuck that. I did a couple of days and nearly went over the edge of a roof in Bermondsey. That was it, no more after that. You never get me up a ladder—no fucking chance. Call the Army, get the fucking Air Force, I ain't going up. But you could change jobs twice a day in them days—lot of work there was, and I was earning all the time. Factories, offices, I was about 10 stone then. Climb through windows, doors, fucking letter-boxes. I was up for anything . . . We did a deal with a butcher when I was on the vans. Had to pick up all the dirty overalls from —— [a supermarket]. We'd go in the back and walk through the warehouse. Geezer there who was in on it, he'd have a lamb or a cotchell [batch] of chickens, maybe a few choice joints of beef in our little trolley, cover up with the shitty overalls, and away. There was loads of little earners like that all the time . . . The word got around that I was up for one and I was earning.

At the age of 17 Danny became engaged to a local woman a year younger than himself, and just weeks later was arrested following an incident outside a dance-hall.

DANNY. It was Sunday night at the Palais—remember rocking up the Palais? I never did it. I come out at closing-time and there was a fight by the bus stop. I was watching, just like you do. Old Bill pulls up, everybody does a runner, and I get a pull. Turns up six months in —— [a detention centre]. Best thing that ever happened to me. In there you have to learn you can't just do what you like. You learn 'Yes sir, no sir.' You wash the floor, and when the screws tread over it you just wash it, don't fucking moan, just do it. Because that's the game. It don't get to you. You just hold it back. Some of the screws were gentlemen. They call you Mr and you called them Sir and it was all right. There was a couple of nasty bastards, like fucking Hitlers, give you a little dig, shout and scream. Just go 'Yes sir, no sir' and then flob [spit] on their backs so they never knew. Walk around with a nice flob running down their back.

Danny emerged from detention centre a wiser man with a clear view of his future.

DANNY. I married Sheil almost straight away. Yeah, she was pregnant like, but we got married anyway . . . I got my licence and was in business straight away. I borrowed a van and just went to work.

Danny made deliveries, went totting, cleared gardens, anything to make a living. He also continued his criminal activities, particularly commercial burglaries and stealing from building-sites.

DANNY. The building was good. In them days there was no security guards—none of that. They might have some old geezer in a little hut. He'd take a stroll round the site then get his head down. There was everything: copper, wood, bricks, paint. If you was careful and took a bit at a time, then you could do it easy, gentle, without the scream going up. There was so much building going on they never noticed. We were doing well. We got a house pretty early on and had holidays, the lot. I bought a van [caravan], put it on a site in Canvey. Then later when I got the HGV I really started to earn. I had a regular earner out at Tilbury and I was doing lorry-loads, moving anything. I went in with Tommy and got a contract with—— [a multiple clothing store]. I nicked their 'received' stamp and we moved lorry-loads. We made thousands, fucking thousands.

CHRIS. Well, he was only doing what everybody else was. You gotta see it from that. I never thought nothing. I suppose when you think back there was always things piled up in the house, people coming and going. I just thought—well, I don't think I did think about it really—it just happened. When you're a kid, as long as everything's all right . . . I suppose I did know it was hookey gear, but when I was out and about with him all it was cartons and boxes, gear moving about, so I never thought about it. What you gotta understand about the old man is he's always said 'Earn money. Don't be a ponce—earn.' And he's always grafted, so that's what you see when you're a kid. That's what I fucking want—bit of graft—some money, fuck it.

By the time Danny was in his mid-thirties times had become tough. He had been through several business partnerships, was deep in debt, and carried several stone overweight as well as half a dozen minor convictions for assault.

DANNY. I had about five really good years, but I pissed it up the wall. I had motors, a couple of lock-ups, spent money boozing like it was yours. I was at it like a good un, always at it. Straight and hookey. If there was any dough the carbuncle on the hip [roll of cash] that is what it all was. I got into some debt with a new unit, but I never thought nothing of it, I was earning so well. Then there was the steel strike. We was doing steel all over the country and it dried up and that, and Andrew [his partner], he was selling gear behind my back. I was out looking for him when he got nicked. While he was away I clocked on to what he was doing—robbing me blind, robbed me blind, the bastard. We had all this gear for the unit. It went missing. Tools, covers, ropes. I was well stitched up. He did me like a kipper.

It was during this difficult period that Chris began to get into trouble, first at school and then on the streets. He became increasingly violent.

CHRIS. I used to love it [school]. I was never no fucking brainbox but first school was nice. The teachers and kids, it was good. Then when I went to the big school it was all 'Stand up straight. Wear a uniform and do as you are told.' I just couldn't handle it. I just got in rows all the time, with other kids as well, but the teachers . . . There was this big mouthy one—he just got into me all the time. I was always having rows with him. Couple of times I just walked out—went home. Then they sent letters and that home, wanting to see Mum and Dad. Then I just went over Wanstead, me and this other kid. We camped out and get into the old lighter fluid. (Laughs.) After a bit they had enough—got barred, kicked out.

DANNY. This school, well, you know what it was, he was too up front. Then he fucks off for the night and I have to go down the nick sign him out. Turns up he's sniffing lighter fuel. So when he goes to —— [a special school] I thought, this will be the making of him. All the kids are the same—fucking awkward, you know—no real villains. Lovely place. Had everything—swimming pool, garages for doing up cars. Then he gets in a ruck with a little mob. He gets charged in court. He gets off it, but after that he went missing a few times, and I give up. I had it up to here. I get bailiffs coming round, then the old bill about him. They loved it 'cos they knew me. 'It's not you this time Mr——. I'm afraid it's your boy again.' I never had two halfpennies not a pot. I'm wheeling, dealing, nowhere. Nothing went right.

When Chris was 14 and in and out of his special school, Danny left home to live with a woman he had had an affair with for a number of years. Chris immediately returned home and assumed the mantle of 'man of the house'.

CHRIS. I had enough of school. It was so fucking boring, all this about 'You break your contract.' Fuck it. I came home. Got a job at ——, the ice-cream place. Said I was 16. I left after about two weeks. They never found out. I just went on the buildings with Tom [his uncle]. Took it from there. He was well at it. He knew all the geezers on the council—give him contracts. I get all cash in hand. Some lovely little fiddles with the others on site. I could get copper, bricks, window-frames; and I was only 14.

Chris moved from job to job over the next two years. The education authorities sent him back to his original local school, but Chris attended for one day before returning to the world of work. Meanwhile, Danny had achieved some kind of reconciliation with his family.

DANNY. I just had it when I went. It was like everything got on top of me. There was no peace. I was doing everything. I chase a pound note all day, came home with 10p— that's what it was like. So Sandi like, I knew her for years. We had a little thing going and I just was over there more and more. I could go there and sit and watch a bit of the box, go over the boozer, game of pool, darts, whatever. Come home, no hassle, no screaming. I needed that . . . I needed that peace and quiet. Then I just sort of drifted back. You know, where she lives, it's just the other side of the square. I mean, I never left them really, not really. I just had to get away. But everything was the same. I knew everybody was all right. Then I suppose I just came back. Still see Sandi like, but I live here again.

By the time Danny returned, Chris had estabished himself as a good earner.

CHRIS. About when I should have left school I had this job as a tyre-fitter. Anything not bald with a bit of tread on it I lobbed over the fence. Picked 'em up later. You know Alex? He had a car lot on —— Road. He'd buy whatever I brought, then he put them on the old motors . . . When he [Danny] came back it never made no odds. I used to see him in the boozer match night. It was all right. Then when he came home it never mattered. I was always out . . . He had this thing about earning and I was earning. He had bits and pieces, then his van got nicked so he was fucked for a bit.

Six months after returning home, Danny became seriously ill and was admitted to hospital.

DANNY. I shit myself. He [the doctor] says 'Well, Mr ——, how much do you drink?' I says 'Not a lot.' He says 'Do you drink spirits?' I says 'Yeah, vodka.' He says 'How much vodka?' So I says 'About a half-bottle.' He says 'That's too much. You must cut it out.' Turns up he thought I meant half a bottle a week. I do that and half a dozen light and bitters a night.

On his return after surgery Danny found himself depressed and physically incapable of hustling for a living. He lost over 3 stone and stopped drinking. Trips to the pub became rare and entire days were spent in front of the TV set. Meanwhile, Chris's entrepreneurial activities were expanding.

DANNY. He stopped getting up in the morning. He was round the house a lot. As long as the dough came he paid his housekeeping. I never bothered. But I knew he was at it, like. He had to be. Not a dabble neither, 'cos he's got himself a little motor and that.

Tension grew during this period. Chris became more confident as Danny's powers waned, and eventually the source of Chris's income became apparent.

DANNY. He's put a pair of jeans in the wash and emptied his pockets out on the table. There's a lump of shit [hash] with his money and that. So I goes in his room and has a look. There's all these deals on his dressing-table. About a dozen little parcels in silver [foil]. I put 'em down the toilet. He comes in and starts banging around. I says 'You looking for something?' He looks at me, so I told him I put it down the fucking toilet. He says 'You bastard. That comes to a lot of money.' I like a bit of a blow myself but not in the fucking house. Why? It ain't right I like a bit of a blow myself but it don't do a right lot. I'd rather have a drink. He starts in the house and that. It's fucking iffy. I ain't having it. You know all about the next thing.

'The next thing' was a fight between Danny and Chris.

CHRIS. I was down a lot of money—I don't know, at least a century (£100)—and I was doubling me money then. I just walked away from him, but he followed me. He just walked behind me. He's giving me all this 'Think you're a big man.' I got by the gate and turned round. He just nutted me.

DANNY. He was gonna have a go, so I got in first, then it was all off. I was still not right, not feeling strong. We whacked each other and fell on the gate. The fucking thing come away from the brick and he hit me with it. I went down and held on to his leg and we finishes up rolling round in the road till the Old Bill got there. Fuckers take him to hospital. Reckons I bit him. Me, I got blood coming out me head. They lock me up for the night.

While Danny was in the police station Chris broke into his lock-up garage and set fire to it. Chris then left home and went to live at his girlfriend's parents' home. While Chris was away, Danny was spasmodically employed delivering smuggled tobacco to outlets in the London area.[2]

DANNY. Been going on for years. I could have been at the beginning when I had the business, but I never reckoned driving abroad. I did boozers, clubs, anything, shops. All Old Holborn it was. I did the Police Club at the back of —— nick, Turned up one day about 3 o'clock—they were fucking legless, even the steward. It was all right, but I knew more about the business than them that was paying me.
CHRIS. After I did the thing with the garage I never went home for a few days, and then just me clothes. I think he [Danny] knew I weren't no little kid he could whack about like he wanted no more. I went back after about three weeks. I got pissed off round Jane's flat. So I just come home. I just never took no notice of him. Just like before I suppose.

While Danny was attempting to impose himself once more upon the market-place, Chris continued to earn, albeit haphazardly, from a variety of sources. Casual employment as a builders' labourer, various driving jobs, dealing in small quantities of dope, and some commercial burglary combined to make a living for a young man who was gaining an increasingly violent reputation. Several local pubs barred him, and he became known to the local police as someone who regularly featured in fights in and around pubs and clubs. At the age of 20 Chris robbed a warehouse of a large quantity of children's clothing.

CHRIS. I put 'em straight out on the markets and that, and people were just turning up outside the house for it. The old man made more than a few phone calls, moved a load of gear through people he knew. Did a load down to somebody he knew, some woman in Dartford. We knocked gear out all over.
DANNY. When I see the cartons and that, had a look at the stuff in them, I thought, this is it, and to be fair he never knew what to do with it. I mean, on a deal I love it. But he was good. He knew he had more than he could handle, so he let me get on with it. Prices—he never had a fucking clue; to be honest with you it was down to me. Like, how big's the parcel? Who are they? They done stuff before? Cash? Sale or return? On this the women were the best 'cos it was all kids' gear. They were having big parcels—£100–£150. Night-time it's 'Here's the money. Let's have some more.' They were just terrific.

At the time both men thrived on the success of their venture. Their familial bond was sealed by a highly successful venture that utilized the resources of youth and maturity to profitable effect. The enterprise boosted Chris's confidence to new heights. He had planned the burglary, paid off accomplices, and dealt in large sums of money for the first time. Most importantly, however, he had been introduced to the intricacies of disposing of a large quantity of stolen goods. The variety of outlets, variations in the sheer bulk of consignments, and the relationship between the perceived personal qualities of buyers, prices, and methods of payment were all crucial elements of the enterprise. The profit from this one act of theft was between £11,000 and £13,000 and Danny was not slow in suggesting how the money should be spent.

DANNY. The lease for the Bulldog [pub] was up, and, let's face it, that had to be mine. It was always coming up. It had a bad reputation. Rough pub, sort of. But I knew I could turn it round, turn it into a family house. But I couldn't get him to put his money into it. If all the dough from the kids' clothes was put into it we was only, what, two grand short. I would have fucking got hold of that somehow. It would have been a pension for him. He could have fucked off and done anything. I would have ran the place. He would have been on wages for fucking ever. No, he's 'Mr Fucking Big'— he's gotta give it that big un. Gotta play gangsters. I know he's not all bad like, but this was a chance to do it properly. He could have still ducked and dived, but a regular earner on business, you can't whack it.

Danny paid off some debts and bought a replacement for his stolen van. Chris invested in a consignment of amphetamine sulphate. He became the co-owner of a second-hand car lot, and a dealer in amphetamines and ecstasy. After less than a year of profitable dealing, he found himself in debt following a successful police operation that led to a number of convictions. Chris found that his drug-dealing activities were in decline, and he turned to a variety of criminal activities merely to pay his bills. As he became more desperate to make a living, be diversified into any activity that promised paper money, and as his desperation increased so did his violence. One night he attacked two men who he claimed owed him money. Danny was in the pub when it happened, and described his son as a 'total fucking animal. No talking, no fucking "Where's the money?" None of that. Just pulled the blade and did 'em.' Danny was never charged for the assault, even though one of his victims has never fully recovered the use of one of his hands.

However, his recklessness did result in increased police interest in his affairs, and for a time Chris was wanted by the police in connection with a minor drugs charge and a credit card fraud. Briefly, his family believed him to be out of the country, but he was in fact living with friends less than ten miles away. During this period Chris went drinking with a cousin and spat into an ashtray while drunkenly playing pool. When the publican told him to leave, Chris hit the man with a bottle and threw a stool at the optics behind the bar, leaving before the police were called. Danny did not hear from him for over six months, during which time Chris's girlfriend gave birth to their first child, a boy.

Meanwhile, Danny has established himself as a supplier of meat pies to pubs and cafés in the area. The pies come from a nearby factory where Danny has a contact, and he claims to be making a living. He even eats the pies himself, but it is difficult to evaluate them as Danny insists on microwaving the cellophane-encased parcels to the consistency of hot, damp polystyrene. We sit in his small kitchen in the early hours, drinking tea and eating pies in an attempt to soak up the previous evening's beer. Now that Chris has left home, I can sleep in what was his bedroom. Danny is explaining the various local scams and feuds that are looming in the coming weeks. The scams feature more pies, and a variation on the ancient 'corner game', which involves selling goods that do not exist to gullible individuals under the pretext that they are buying stolen property. The feuds relate to combustible pockets of savagery that erupt with little warning every few years. Danny is contemplating a visit from a cousin who has recently been released from prison. Whenever they meet they drink, and whenever they drink they fight. On the subject of Chris, it is rumoured that he is again dealing in drugs, and he is in the process of setting up home with his new family. Danny insists that his son will one day make a lot of money and learn to keep it. 'All he needs is a good slap.'

Danny and Chris have successfully maintained their identities by plucking violence from a catalogue of cultural precedents, and reworking them in conjunction with commercial practice. Business serves as a master metaphor for the competent application of money-making strategies siphoned through a fine gauze of manly pursuits. While the future for Danny and Chris is uncertain, Chris's 6-month-old son has a brand new building society book and a tiny pair of red leatherette boxing-gloves.

3

Hard Man: Jimmy's Story

The day his father died, Jimmy spent the day vomiting. He was in the first three months of a four-year sentence for grievous bodily harm, and his body had yet to adapt to the rigours of prison cuisine.

I come off the hospital wing, and the screw says that I'm wanted in the principal's office. I just tells him that I ain't going nowhere. I couldn't fucking move, felt so fucking rank. So he says 'All right, your father's dead.' That's all he was going to say. That was that. He weren't having a go, nothing like that. He just thought that was the right thing to do, like telling me last night's football. Never took it in at first like, I just lie there retching. Then the geezer I'm banged up with comes in with a fucking great plate of some shit they was serving up. Geezer's out of Watford or Cheshunt or somewhere. Starts whacking this stuff down his neck with a spoon, and all the time he's talking to me. But I don't, I can't, hear him, all I can see is this white stuff . . . some fucking slimy shit slobbering all over his mouth.

Then I clocks on he's on about his old man, and he never really knew him and all that old bollocks. And going on and on, and then I suss it what the screw said. Now nothing against him, but he had to get out the fucking cell or I was going to kill him. All this you read about being inside, I read all them books—you know, us against them, taking on the system—it's bollocks. You get the old boys. They all reckon they knew the Krays, all the real fucking stars. They read the books and there's the film; and the McVicar film, that's another one. They talk about it like it's a fucking boys' club, like *Porridge* on the telly. Hard men, funny men, all taking on the system. It ain't like that. If we was all the same, like all in for violence, then, I suppose, then McVicar it might be true. But not now, most of 'em are just losers, kids, car thieves, fucking car thieves and smellies. Old drunks come in to clean up . . . You get a few old weekend gangsters talking about how back when the twins were about nobody grassed and that, but it's like when your mum goes on about the good old days, it's all like memory and that . . .

All I know is that when things go wrong inside there ain't no fucker gonna help. So I says to this geezer 'No offence, Brian, but if you don't walk out that fucking door I will kill you.' Now the geezer is no fucking mug. But he looks at me and just goes, no questions. Next morning probation officer comes in. Heart attack, died indoors. I put in for special leave but I never got out for the funeral. When I got my next visit I found out what occurred.

Jimmy hospitalized his first opponent while still at primary school. A routine playground scuffle between Jimmy and a classmate became more serious, and the classmate spent several days in hospital. The green shoots of his reputation as a hard man sprung from his use of a rubbish bin as a weapon.

Never a thing really. Like I was the only boy in the family . . . sisters sort of push you about, like bully, but gentle. But I got cousins and they're all local. All fighters, they were. Soon as I got big enough to play out I was out rucking, like running about with them, and thinking about it now, I suppose, well, I know fighting, it's not how you should go about things, but like they was rough people, and you had to be rough too. I mean, we was always fighting with anybody. School, street, it's like a way of life really. And you could never cry, never cry. You just go mental, hurt people. Sometimes I was frightened though, like if somebody was really hurt.

Once we was playing in the old school, and something was off and we was out— caretaker come or something. We all got out the playground, over the fence—over the big metal gate. This kid goes under it. It was on a slope and we all did it. Your head could just squeeze under it, and one little kid was just getting under, and as his head is just sort of wedged under the metal, my cousin, the oldest one, Ricky, he ran at him and kicked him in the side of the head. He was only a little kid, 8 or 9, and we thought he was dead. We run anywhere and when we looked round he was just there, not moving with his head stuck under the metal. We all did things like that, and you just did it, no questions.

This kid, the little kid, they took him to hospital. . . . His dad come in the playground few days later. We was playing football and he goes up to Ricky to give him a slap. Ricky just lashes out with a pump, bike pump. First time I ever see a boy fight a man. He was about 17, no, less, 14, 15, and he held his own till the geezer got hold of him, slapped him about . . . Ricky, I don't think he lives round here. He went Africa or, yeah, worked as a, like in a casino. Did come back . . . pisshead, don't know, somewhere.

Jimmy's father was the first of a long line of tinkers to settle down into regular employment. His ancestors feature prominently in the folk memories of many elderly residents of north and east London. They bought and sold scrap metal, old gold, jewellery, horses, and more recently cars and lorries. They were renowned as street fighters and drinkers, and for the manner in which, during the Second World War, every adult male in the family disappeared for the duration. Jimmy's father had spent the war as a 'wardrobe dealer', buying and selling second-hand clothes.[1] Just after the war Jimmy's father became eligible for the armed services, but was rejected on rather dubious health grounds (as was one of Jimmy's uncles, who was a prominent fairground-booth boxer).

He was the first one to settle, like a real, what you might call a proper job working for another person, not just like family. . . . Why? Never said. He did get married young, so that might have something to do with it. . . . Suppose he wanted something regular.

Two of Jimmy's uncles went on to become wealthy men, one as a scrap-metal dealer, the other as a south coast property developer and estate agent. However, the remainder of this vast family continued to survive on the margins of normative economic activity.

We were the only ones with a house. The others were always moving about, so they come to our house a lot. I never thought of it at the time, but the place was always full of kids and the old man did shift work . . . Some of my uncles and that, they was working away, and when the kids were old enough to go to school, they got prefabs down from us, so we ended up all in the same school.

By the time Jimmy moved on to secondary school at the age of 11, he had forged a formidable reputation as a fighter, a reputation enhanced by the brutal potential of his large extended family. Families offered protection, education, and the possibility of retribution. For although Jimmy came from a family of girls, he was bonded by violence to his cousins, and would reaffirm his commitment to them by whatever means necessary.

There was what, eight, ten of us? And we would all back each other up. But that was the way it was then—everybody was in big families. So if two kids started a little row, they all got into one. Big brothers, sisters, mums and dads, old people. If you never had that back-up, specially brothers or, like I had, then, well . . .[2] At school we was murders. Front up the teachers. We run the place. But not the headmaster. He was a big man, bald, with dark, like, sunglasses. They said he had to wear them—got in a fight years back with some kids—Teddy Boys who was at the school. . . . Done all of 'em. He was the only one. Once they shoved the piano down the stairs, started fires in the class. We all had knives, it was the thing, just fucking about. . . . Boy got stabbed in my last year. One who did it was like with us, me and my cousins. He was put away, and I remember thinking 'Fuck that, that could have been me.' The thought of it, prison like, or borstal, it was the one thing like that made me wonder . . . what's it about? But you keep out of it, you don't think it can really happen, and we just kept on. Started earning.

WE WAS MURDERS

The nearest thing to a family business was a scaffolding firm run by one of Jimmy's uncles.

Good money, good money. Out and about a lot, mainly family like. My family, cousins and that, they was all on the firm. . . . Come and go. It was good, and we had a good time, all of us. We earnt well and night-time we was all out. We was faces, you know, known faces. . . . If you took us on, it was all of us, and you had to go for a real result with us. We took places over. Pubs and that, the bouncers—nothing. We knew all of them, so they never bothered. If we had a row we dealt with it, then that was it, over.

By the time he was 19 years old Jimmy, his cousins, and their associates were being asked by the landlords of 'trouble pubs' to frequent their premises.

How? Just happened. I don't know, word got about that we could like do the business. Thing is I would get right up front if there was a ruck. I would be right up there. You had to, it was . . . it was what you had to do. We'd fight anybody, and with us, what you got, it was like hospital, serious. . . . People knew with us it was all off. We was murders.

Jimmy, his cousins and their ever growing entourage were increasingly regarded as calming influences by the landlords of trouble pubs, and were welcomed wherever violence blighted business. One such pub was owned by an ex-policeman, who in the first couple of years of his retirement experienced little trouble from rowdy or violent customers. However, his reluctance to remain open twenty-four hours a day in order to quench the thirsts of his ex-colleagues, and a growing reputation for rowdy behaviour, including drag acts and strip-tease shows that 'got out of hand', led to a decline in the number of police customers. The pub, physically isolated and deprived of its best customers, plunged rapidly into decline as the landlord neglected his business in order to concentrate on his golf.

Everybody remembers that when it happened. I know an Old Bill, and it's what all them years he still talks about it. The girls behind the bar like, we knew them, and we paid for everything, but it was—get a round in and we get charged half-price. He [the landlord] never said nothing, but he knew, he had to. But we was good. There was never no trouble when we was having a drink. I don't know what it was, this night it just blew. Peter had a row so they reckon, but first thing I knew there's a crash, furniture and screaming and that. We all get there and he's on the floor, face down, and the blood is just sort of steady. It's steady . . . and it's just steady coming out.

The young man died there on the pub's linoleum floor. His assailant had escaped in the ensuing chaos, and was arrested within the hour hiding nearby. He was convicted of manslaughter, and the trial judge described the case as a tragedy.

Everybody loved him, Peter. He was the biggest of all of us like, but he weren't no bother to nobody. Still got no idea what it was all about. Geezer hit him with a glass and it broke. Cut his throat open and that was that, fucking dead.

The high profile of the case and his close proximity to the butchery established Jimmy irrevocably as one of the violent élite.

The boy what did it got put away. Then in the papers it started all this about his family getting threats and that. They all moved out the area, I don't know where or nothing, but they went . . . Then when we got anywhere . . . they'd stand back out the way just like we did it, like we topped him. After that nobody fucked about with us, and we played on it, all started getting tooled up when we went out. I was still on the scaffolding and so was the others, either that or the building. . . . Once we all put our belts on under our jackets, like scaffolding belts with all the tools round them. We waited for a little ruck to start and we was off. All the tools come out and we was into them. We used anything then. But as we were all together, all in a little mob, then nobody could touch us.

Soon they were able to graduate beyond free drinks, and started to earn hard cash in exchange for high visibility at pubs and clubs around the neighbourhood. Violence by now was rare. Their presence was normally enough to impose an aura of control. Yet when it was used it was so extreme that the attentions of the police became inevitable. Jimmy was arrested after two men were stabbed and badly beaten at a disco.

We had the bar area and the two dance-floors. How it worked was we never took the door—that was down to the proper bouncers, like them with the suits and that. We was there to back all them up, but we just got on with it, just run it for us. We got £150 about and we never paid for nothing. They come up on a lift from the door and that took them into the bar, and that's when you got them. Anybody wants a row, we are there for them.

They know who we are and where we are. I don't know what it was that night, but it was late and two of ours was chatting up two sorts. Little mob has a few words with them and it's all off.

We did them, all the way down in the lift and out the front, but one went down the side stairs and me and Alan goes down and gets him by the fire door. I never even had a screwdriver what they reckon they was done with, just a piece of plumbers' metal wrapped round me hand. The two what was stabbed was in the lift and come out the front, but I got tugged in the Indian [restaurant] about an hour later. It must have been the manager of the place. He was getting the fucking hump about us, but he come to us and he got his money's-worth 'cos there was us what earnt from it, and then there was all our mates who just come for the ruck.

That did it, even when they dropped it [the case] my card was marked and I started to get pulled regular. It got so the old man had enough of it and slung me out. He was always coming home from work in the mornings, and the Old Bill be on the doorstep with the fucking milk waiting to give me a pull. Got so I never went out for fear of being anywhere near a ruck.

After a brief period Jimmy returned home and started to come to terms with a violent reputation that now brought him into regular contact with the police. Still only in his late teens offers of criminal work started to come his way.

When someone's got some work, all you can do is sort out what the geezer's like. Like, who knows him, what's he done before, and that. I was getting little whispers all the time through the family about work, but I never bothered. I was only a kid. I never knew nothing. . . . I was earning well on the scaffolding, earning of a night. I give my mum me housekeeping and that was that. I only had me prick to keep. . . . So some old face comes up and starts sounding out about a blag, shooters and that. I never took it in; you don't when you're that age. You don't look, you don't want to be bothered. Anyway, they were old geezers, and I just wanted to have a good time with me cousins.

At the age of 21, after numerous encounters with the police, Jimmy received his first custodial sentence, and found himself contemplating the prospect of two years in a shared cell, far from the pubs and clubs that had been contributing an ever-increasing proportion of his income. Jimmy was curiously reluctant to talk about his time in prison, despite his enthusiasm for talking about his business and in particular his family and their involvement in the various enterprises that marked his early adult life. Prison was not an experience that Jimmy valued; indeed he seemed to despise the sentimental reminiscences of the 'old lags'. Yet prison and the maturity it brought did change Jimmy's attitude to his prospects. His cousins and their cohorts had started to settle into long-term relationships, and several had started families.

I went back on the scaffolding and started earning, and there was a lot of travel—overnights and that. . . . Well, it was different. They was the same as before but married, some of them, and they wasn't about as much. . . . I was away most of the week, back of a Friday usually, but with the wives and that it was different. I don't know what it was but I suppose as they got older they sort of drifted, and they weren't so bothered about going out. We could still earn. There was a boozer on the island, he [the landlord] was a pal of my uncles and he loved us. Whenever we went in there—drink, everything, was nothing. He used to get fish out the old Billingsgate; we had oysters, lobsters, everything in there. My mate Danny had his stag-night in there, got pissed, fell asleep on the seats. We got this ugly bastard fish out the fridge, put it down his trousers with the head poking out his flies. (Laughs.)

Not like before; it was different. We still had the 'Rooms' of a Friday and if there was a special on, but we never went out as much, not all together. (Long pause.) People started to get married—that was one thing. Then there was me getting put away. They never said nothing, but, well, we got away with it for so long it was a like 'pull in your horns'. We still rucked all the time, but nothing serious, and if somebody asked us—well, the geezer, like I said before, what had the place on the island. Any problems then we go down and just drink in there for a bit and make ourselves at home. There was a few quid here and there but . . .

When he was 23 Jimmy married a woman twelve years his senior, a divorcée who owned several clothing-shops and an employment agency in a small commuter town about two hours' drive from London. They had met when Jimmy worked on the renovation of a large country property adjacent to a pub where he stayed during the week. Elaine was one of the pub's regulars, and soon Jimmy had moved into her comfortable home, seldom returning to London. His mother died of cancer, and within three months Jimmy and Elaine married quietly at her local registry office. Jimmy's father was the only member of his family present; there was no stag-night, and there was no trace of what should have been a traditional London working-class wedding.

I only went back when I had to. I tried to make it like different. There was a lot of work down there as it happened, so I put myself about and it was all right. Doing building and that, plenty of work. . . . We was having holidays, I mean she shut one of the shops but she was a very shrewd woman and we had a good life. . . . I suppose I had enough of it. . . . I wanted to settle down, wanted a place of me own. I mean if anything come up, I still had to know about it. Like with any snides [counterfeit notes] or bits of gear, but I never went to work, I never got involved. I mean she had her business and I never wanted to naus it up.

CRIME FLIES

Elaine owned an apartment on a Mediterranean tourist island, and the couple were frequent vacationers, even spending their first Christmas together there. Jimmy loved the island and decided to invest in a small bar, going into partnership with a builder from the Midlands who had retired to the sun some years earlier. Jimmy's friends and family took full advantage of free accommodation whenever he and Elaine were in England, and the bar became the focal point of their stay.

Jimmy, still working as a self-employed scaffolder and roofer, found that he was having to travel ever farther afield to get work. This often meant overnight stopovers, which in turn fostered resentment from Elaine, who had bought the house next door to the bar with a view to converting it into a restaurant. After they had been married for about two years, Jimmy received a telephone call from the Birmingham builder's wife pleading with him to fly to the island as her husband had been arrested. Jimmy's friends and former colleagues had been using the bar as an outlet for counterfeit notes, changing thousands of pounds into local currency. Jimmy never returned to his island in the sun, and a rift developed between him and his wife that would never heal.

It was down to Sammy. As soon as I heard, well, I never had to go looking for him— he came to me. Up front he was, gives me two grand. I never give him a slap. I got Elaine to go out and get rid of the bar, but she couldn't move it. She come back and we had this bar, this like bar in the corner of the living-room. She smashed it up. It was too much for her, all the aggravation. I think her business was a bit iffy too. She slung me out, to be honest, and it weren't working out, so I come home.

She sold up. I let it go, like never see none of it. It was in her name so fuck it. The other one [the builder], he came out of it all right. They just let him go, I think. He never knew what it was about. . . . Elaine, after we got a divorce, she got a boozer out somewhere. Died of cancer when I was away the last time.

Jimmy returned to London and lived with his father, who, following his wife's death, had sought solace in whisky. One of Jimmy's cousins had started a minicab firm in the suburbs, and recruited several family members on a cash-in-hand basis both to drive and to supervise other drivers. It was during this period that Jimmy became acquainted with armed robbery.

We always talked about it, you know, like if you could get away with it, what to do with the dough. Then we just got started. There was a load of stuff going on round then with the cabs, like if you was going on another firm's plot and that. We had a motor burnt out and phone calls, so we kept a sawn-off under the counter. Then that was that. Really we just went to work.

GOING TO WORK

By the time he was 28 Jimmy was a rich man. With the proceeds of a number of armed robberies he became a part-owner of a newsagent's, two pubs, and a caravan site on the south coast. He is unwilling to engage with either the existential self-reflections of the superstar robbers or the cosy quasi-Dickensian blag-speak of the retired villainry.

It was easy. I think about it now and it's like, we just went out and robbed. We never planned nothing and we never really worked nothing out.

I objected that he must have planned things like the target and who did what.

Why? All it is is somebody says you want the work? Well —— [bank] looks tasty and . . . What you don't fucking realize or don't want to fucking realize, we ain't fucking mad geniuses all plotting up work and that. You just go in and take the fucking money. Pure and simple. . . . I mean, what you fucking expect? All fucking mean and moody, all plans and months of plans and that.[3] . . . I ain't saying it's easy—you must want it. It's fucking obvious when you go in a place you get people to do as you fucking tell them. Either that or there's no point. But so fucking what? It's like anything you do. There's no trick to it. You go in hard, you get the money and fuck off.

Jimmy was unwilling to elaborate further, but through interviews with friends, family, and former colleagues it became apparent that Jimmy was known as a 'good worker' who was trustworthy and could be relied upon to act resourcefully in tight situations. Most importantly, he avoided capture, marking him out as someone who could successfully ply his trade without implicating himself or others. Jimmy worked with a number of teams operating mainly in the Home Counties during the mid-1970s. The robberies were largely unspectacular—almost mundane in both the choice of target and execution. I asked why he never got arrested.

(Sigh.) I just didn't. I was careful, but so was some of the others, and it did come on top for some of them. I never got grassed, and I never worked with any of them that topped up grassing. But I knew some of them who did. I don't know, I just did good work; that and I never shot nobody. I never even fired the fucking thing.[4]

Jimmy remained a marketable resource for some time, even after he was badly injured in a stabbing at a drinking-club. The stabbing was the result of an argument between one of Jimmy's cousins and a man suspected of having an affair with his wife.

In drink, what I remember of it. Nobody except them two wanted it, and they was at each other a couple of times when we was inside. It was the time we had a result with the cash and carries, and we never needed drawing attention to us. But they kept at it, but we kept just pulling them apart. Then when we was looking for a cab it was all off. I don't remember too much, but I was leaning on a wall holding the blood in on me guts, and they was all running. Then it was hospital.

Jimmy almost died of his wounds, and it was nearly a year before he was able to work again. By this time armed robbery as a profession was in decline. During his convalescence Jimmy met a teacher who worked in a local primary school, and they set up home in a rented flat in a suburb next to his old neighbourhood. He had considerable funds coming in from his legitimate businesses. By the time of the stabbing he was well established as a robber and was able to be choosy about his work, selecting targets likely to give the maximum return.

Soon after Jimmy's come-back he was arrested at his new home, only to be released with an assurance that 'Your turn has come.' Until then Jimmy had received little professional attention from the police, although several CID officers were among his regular drinking partners. Now he found himself as one of the usual suspects rounded up after every armed robbery committed in London and the Home Counties. Early-morning raids became routine, and he stopped driving his car as he had also become a target for vigilant uniformed officers. Eventually the pressure on his new relationship proved too much, and his partner moved out. Within a few months Jimmy moved back in with his father, returning to the back bedroom of his boyhood home. But the money kept rolling in.

Jimmy is agnostic on the subject of policing. It was difficult to draw him out on any issues relating to police work, and he considered my interest in the subject to be totally misplaced. For Jimmy the police are at best an irrelevance, and at worst an obstruction. They had little influence on his day-to-day existence, posing few problems, and inspiring little more than mild caution on his behalf. They are only important if you are caught, and getting caught has little to do with guilt and still less to do with justice. Jimmy paid more attention to his legitimate business interests.

In the late 1980s he was convicted for stabbing a man, a builder with whom he had struck up a potentially lucrative arrangement involving the theft and recycling of building materials. A contact working for a local authority would deliberately order goods that were surplus to requirements, and channel the surplus into the business operated by Jimmy and the builder. In this way the business was able to undercut all local competition and it quickly got itself established, particularly with developers wishing to reroof or double-glaze their properties. The builder's brother, a roofer, took his Doberman to work with him, leaving the dog in his van while he climbed ladders with tiles stacked on his head. He was recognized to be a particularly volatile man, with a record of extreme violence.

There were numerous disputes involving the roofer, who was self-employed. Resolution was usually reached when the builder handed over large wads of cash, and it was inevitable that Jimmy would eventually intervene. When the confrontation did occur it had a rather unexpected outcome. The roofer was working on a house in the suburbs when, as arranged with the builder, Jimmy arrived to tell the man that his rates were too high and his services would no longer be required. The argument was brief and the obligatory fight somewhat truncated. The roofer went down and Jimmy followed through, only to find himself being attacked by his business partner, the builder. As Jimmy turned his attentions to his attacker, the roofer ran to his van and released the Doberman, which, instead of attacking Jimmy as commanded, bounded down the street and disappeared into a nearby park. As the roofer set off in pursuit of his dog, Jimmy stabbed the builder in the chest and buttocks.

STEAMING

The Turkish baths on a Friday afternoon were the one part of Jimmy's routine that was non-negotiable. He would arrive just after noon, and steadily work his way through the four rooms that are graduated by heat, from the soothing balm of the 'dry room', to the eyelash-singeing, lung-searing intensity of 'number 4'. The baths offer an endearing picture of males working hard at their leisure. Bodies are scoured, scraped, soaped, and lightly flagellated. They are silently baked in a number of variations, as young men stretch, old athletes perform press-ups, and newcomers fret over the correct response to offers of 'an all-over soaping'.

The routines are ritualistic and heavily coded. Small co-operatives of cleansers work silently, alternatively foaming and sluicing, before dispatching their charges to the needle-sharp power-showers, and the chore of purification is reciprocated. At the centre of this steamy temple of hygiene stands the Beast. Short, squat, and with his long grey hair tied back in a pony-tail, the Beast wears a minuscule towel around a girth that appears to quake at irregular intervals. His long beard is plaited over the heavy gold chain that hangs around his neck, and his industrial-weight Wellington boots encase legs vividly mapped with varicose veins.

The Beast runs the still centre of the baths at a stone altar, and it is upon this altar that anyone with a £5 note is sacrificed to the relentless attentions of the Beast's massage. Jimmy pays the Beast £10 and, by the time he lowers himself agonizingly slowly into the ice-cold plunge pool, has been pummelled pink by a man who, some say, received the cat-o'-nine-tails while in prison during the early 1950s, and, others maintain, learnt his craft while languishing in a North Korean prison camp. Either way, the Beast had the power in his vast steely mitts to send Jimmy, now wrapped in towels, into the rest-room fit for little more than two poached eggs on toast, a quick game of brag, and a nap.

The rest-room functions most crucially as a market-place where goods, services, and ideas can be exchanged in an atmosphere of *bonhomie* and relative trust. Like all gentlemen's clubs, the leisure options are strictly prescribed, although members are licensed to bullshit at will. Yet skilled operators are experienced at teasing gems from the mire, and Jimmy carefully selects his company so as to mix business with pleasure judiciously. The Turkish bath is a place of elaborate performance, where individuals go naked into a world enhanced by steam, and tales of the pub, and the backs of lorries are skilfully arranged to enhance reputations that could suffer were they exposed to the cold chill of the street.

While two men place bets on the eating abilities of Warren, Jimmy shows little interest in two other conversations that are spinning not quite out of control. He pays more attention, as do most of the clientele, to the small black man who has one minute to consume as many Jacob's biscuits as possible without taking a drink. This weekly ritual is vital for Jimmy to maintain his status. For as a local 'face' he must be seen to be active, involved, delving for information, and displaying the kind of cultural competence that can win £20 on a packet of dry biscuits.

However, for Jimmy the world can never remain benign for long, and confirmation that life is a maelstrom of malevolence tends to recur with tedious regularity. In the changing-room Jimmy dries himself and puts on his street clothes. As he combs his damp hair a naked man some 6 inches taller and 30 pounds heavier is searching aggressively for a bottle of shampoo, kicking lockers and slamming doors. Eventually he focuses upon Jimmy, who is facing away, apparently absorbed in the final stage of the afternoon's body maintenance, which involves draping strands of hair over a bald spot at the crown of his head. By now the changing-room is crowded with men intent upon exorcising the working week from their minds and bodies, before the drinking can begin. The leisured élite who have languished here all afternoon are leaving, lest they are contaminated by the world of work. The weekend started here, but the atmosphere drains the changing-room of its usual festive euphoria. 'Where's my fucking shampoo?' is murmured into the back of Jimmy's skull, as other customers pay immediate attention to their shoes and the insides of their holdalls. 'You got it?' The man steps closer and points to a fat young man dressed in a towel and a pair of flip-flops. 'You saw him, you said. Yeah?' Flip-flop nervously grunts his agreement, but appears extremely uncomfortable at being drawn into the rapidly escalating situation. Jimmy continues to arrange his hair and quietly utters 'I've not got it.' The man steps closer and Sammy the towel-collector stops to watch. 'You fucking got it. Give me yours.' It's now beyond saving and Jimmy turns. He appears to be in pain, as if the stress of the situation is too much to bear. His head, hands, and feet blur, and he drives the man, whose nakedness suddenly seems pathetic, into the lockers. He would probably have slumped to the floor, but Jimmy's blows pin him up. When he finally goes down, Jimmy stamps on his shoulder and the side of his face. I didn't see the blow that split Jimmy's lip. He merely wiped it with a towel as he picked up his holdall and walked out.

Real violence, as opposed to its fictional facsimile, has an intensity and desperation that is far removed from gladiatorial endeavour, with its formularized repertoires. Similarly, pugilistic skill or knowledge of martial arts are unlikely to enhance performance. Certainly without extreme ferocity, such knowledge can even be counter-productive. There is no room for restraint, no opportunity for mercy. Neither are there points for style or mock aggression: a pulled punch is no punch at all. When people like Jimmy fight they are out to inflict maximum damage, and there can be little doubt that if Jimmy's comb had been made of steel he would have used it to stab his opponent.

Jimmy is committed to violence. Violence sustains his identity as a man who, within the parameters of entrepreneurial criminality, demands total respect. He is unable to compromise—for this would be to remove the very essence of self. Every semblance of his being is packed into a framework of confrontational options which are manifested as violent potential. Jimmy defines himself in terms of a cultural inheritance that gives primacy to violence, and his willingness to embrace whole-heartedly his inheritance marks him out from others whose daily strategies feature the avoidance of conflict.

Jimmy's father was one such man who, despite his background, was the antithesis of the uncompromising villain. A family man who worked hard on the railways for most of his life, he died alone after falling downstairs at home, and it was several days before Jimmy's eldest sister discovered the body. Jimmy now lives with one of his sisters and her young family in the suburbs, close to the pub that is now his only apparent source of income. Recently there was a shooting in the pub's car park. He has a room above the garage, and when he drives to work in the morning his 3-year-old niece waves goodbye to a man who remains committed to violence.

4

Fat Boys

The Fat Boys' car lot boasts no lavatory that conforms to twentieth-century sensibilities. Consequently, Fat Laurie has learnt to delay his early-morning bowel movement till pub opening-time, and at 11 a.m. precisely, six days a week, he crosses the main road to enjoy a shit and a Scotch in the tranquil environs of the Dog. It is in this alcoholic dawn, where pine disinfectant battles with stale tobacco smoke and the phantoms of last night's beer, before the gaming-machine is illuminated, that Fat Laurie gives me his philosophy of life. We had been silently drinking coffee in his office when he had exclaimed 'Going for a shit. Coming?'

I ain't a villain, never have been. The motors is straight. I do deals with anybody gonna put money in me pocket, but everybody does that. I look at it this way: it's Friday afternoon. All week I ain't sold a fucking bean. I got the VAT and the tax on me back for money I haven't got. I got a little sort I'm supposed to see later on and the wife's in me ear. In my pocket I got nothing. I'm lending sandwich money off that old cunt who washes the motors. Then in comes some punter, not a mug, ordinary geezer like yourself, maybe out for a bit of a bargain. But when you come in I make up my mind that whatever money is in your pocket I have to have it 'cos I am desperate.

An hour later I've done a cash deal for money and everything's sweet. It don't matter if Monday morning you come back screaming that there's no fucking engine whatever. I give you a cheque 'cos it's not worth the—fuck it, customer's always right and that. I just start all over again and I've had a loan of your money over the weekend.

The three Fat Boys have owned the car lot for over a decade. They run it from an old shop next to the site of a demolished building and the rows of high mileage, ex-sales reps cars are framed by the faded outlines of stairways, fireplaces, and mantelpieces, the detritus of a long-dead domestic order.

Laurie and his brother Stan run the business. They have been in the motor trade most of their lives, and at one stage in the early eighties operated three car lots specializing in redundant fleet vehicles. As the recession bit the Fat Boys suffered. Laurie was convicted for his minor role in a major fraud, and after serving two years found that his wife had left him and that Fat Boys Inc. was down to one car lot. He took up golf and married a divorcée with her own hairdressing business. Much to Stan's consternation Laurie regularly smokes dope in the office, and there is frequent confusion when one of Laurie's girl-friends is allowed to borrow a car from the lot. He looks like a bucolic golf pro in his primary colours, immaculately coiffed hair, and gold-buckled casuals. He might have been transported from some super-affluent Euro-resort. However, his aura of relaxed well-being owes more to Moroccan black than to good news from his broker received while on the way to a discreet lunch in the hills above Marbella, before eighteen holes with Sean Connery.

Stan doesn't play golf and in marked contrast to his younger brother has a formal sense of style that complements his sense of business decorum. Stan favours a sports jacket, shirt, and tie, addresses customers as Sir or Madam, and has a prostate problem that does not allow him to share his younger brother's squeamishness about their unsanitary toilet facilities. Fat Stan spends a lot of time at auctions buying stock and disposing of vehicles taken in part-exchange. He takes the business very seriously, and objects to his brother's leisurely attitude. No matter what the weather is like outside, if Laurie lights up a joint, Stan opens the door and all the windows, and then stands out on the car lot checking the stock until his brother has finished smoking. Laurie confided to me his wonderment when on the day of their mother's funeral, Stan was back at the office by mid-afternoon to catch any trade that might drop in from the passing rush-hour.

But business has been slack for some time, and, as Laurie practises his swing, Stan works hard on the telephone.

You won't get cheaper. If you make me an offer, and I'm gonna say this to you just so you know, if you make me an offer, it's got to be close. We had it there so long we put it down to that as a give-away.... You fucking killing me.... No, I can't do it, our mark-up on that won't pay the weekly phone bill. You're taking the piss—you know that. What are you, the fucking Revenue?

The two Fat Boys like to eat. They eat all day and they eat anything that they can lay their hands on. In the morning they arrive at work with food, and very soon afterwards go to the café next door for their breakfast. The café used to provide breakfasts and lunches for the primarily labouring workforce in the neighbourhood, but now it is a snack-bar owned by a former chemical worker who invested his redundancy money into a long lease, a Formica refit, a frying-pan, and a microwave oven. Laurie and Stan bring their food back to the office where they have their own bottle of ketchup and eat on the hoof. Double pie and chips heated in the microwave is a particular favourite, along with bacon sandwiches, sausage and chips, and fried egg rolls. By lunch-time they look further afield for sustenance and bring back fish and chips. (Stan removes the batter and gives it to Laurie, who regards it as something of a delicacy). Every Friday is double pie and mash. Frequent visits to the microwave next door for afternoon snacks top them up before their colossal lager intake begins at around 5.30.

The third Fat Boy never seems to eat anything and seldom comes into the office. Peter is unrelated to the other two Fat Boys, and has a repair workshop at the back of the car lot just the other side of a narrow service road that is always jammed with cars awaiting his attentions. He works alone. Even bigger than his partners, Peter is permanently covered in oil and grease. His T-shirts, which he changes occasionally, hardly look any different whether they are fresh or dirty—everything is faded to grime. His camouflage trousers are perfectly complemented by the ancient boots, which after years of hard wear now reveal a glint of steel from the toe-cap.

Peter's world is one of grinders, drills, and sanders. To an unrelenting background of country music emanating from a portable cassette-player, Peter specializes in bodywork, but is happy to take on any mechanical task. He gets the cars that Stan buys from auction into vendible condition, and as most of the cars that he renovates are sold on through the trade before they reach the car lot, his back-street operation is crucial.

Relationships between Fat Peter and the two big eaters can often be fraught. When the back-street gets busy, Peter puts cars on the main road and employs a young Asian man to assist him. The noise generated by the kerbside bodywork Stan finds especially irritating, and when Peter comes into the office he finds Stan complaining to the young man whom Laurie has christened YTS.

STAN. I know it's a drill, you cunt; it's not a fucking hoover. How do I do business?
PETER. It's a sander.
STAN. A what?
PETER. A sander.
STAN. Oh, that's all right then. How do I do business?
PETER. It is business, this is what it is. He's earning. The last thing you moved was your arsehole over the pub.

Peter can get any part for a Ford within twenty-four hours. His contacts at the factory are so extensive that he established himself several years ago as a major dealer of black-market car parts. About ten years ago he bought a smallholding, where he keeps chickens, a couple of horses, and several outbuildings full of car parts. He is proud of his rural existence, shoots rabbits at weekends, and has built a number of go-karts for his teenage son. But his rural life-style offers more than a relief from ducking and diving in the urban wasteland, for the space and anonymity of the countryside also affords green-field opportunities.

SLAUGHTER

It became apparent that Peter was managing only one, albeit crucial, aspect of a wider operation. His relationship with the other Fat Boys was important, but hardly accounted for the constant flow of traffic through his back-street workshop. Any-time that I attempted to move our conversation on to criminality beyond the second-hand car business or black-market car parts, he would just smile and gently but firmly change the subject. The latter was a lucrative activity but, for Peter at least, required no explanation. But when Mickey walked into the pub one evening after work, it quickly became obvious that the senior partner had arrived.

The Fat Boys were also operating as agents for an occasional 'slaughter' at a remote industrial estate close to Peter's country seat. Thieves considering the prospect of an entire lorry- or container-load of stolen goods needed a discreet spot for the distribution of the loot, and Mickey's warehouse was ideally situated. Peter had got to know him through a fishing-club, and as they also shared an interest in motor vehicles, a link was forged between the Fat Boys' premises and Mickey's outpost in the entrepreneurial badlands. Thieves like Robin[1] respect the businesslike nature of the arrangement, and periodically used the slaughter's facilities and any necessary labour via the Fat Boys' front office.

I never have nothing to do with this Mickey. I see Peter or one of the others to get things sorted. I tell 'em what it is, and when it's coming, and what I need and that. . . . They tell me what it comes to. If it's just a straight in and out with no extras, labour or nothing, then that's easy. If I need storage, then its more, and sometimes when I tell 'em what it is one of 'em might start placing stuff for me. So of course it all costs.

Mickey liked the idea of talking to me about his career. Peter's sneering introduction included the line 'some fucking teacher or something', and this made me safe. We arranged to meet at his office at the slaughter, and I got a lift from YTS, who was dropping off some decorating materials. YTS, if he knew the full extent of the Fat Boys' criminal involvement, gave no sign of it. He was paid by the day to carry out any odd jobs that needed doing around the car lot, and taking me and a van-load of paint down to Mickey's was just another chore.

The barrier was already raised and the security guard sitting in his sentry-box by the gate barely looked up as we drove through the entrance. Mickey's office was at the top of a row of delivery bays rented by different firms, and as we backed into Mickey's bay the only other commercial vehicle on the site pulled out. YTS placed the cans of paint on to the deserted loading-bank, while Mickey made coffee. The office was sparse, furnished only with a pile of cellophane-wrapped telephone directories on a self-assembly desk. Apart from a calendar on the wall from a stationery supply company, there were none of the trappings of a modern office. After dismissing YTS with £10 for a 'drink', Mickey was keen to commence our interview; so keen that when I took the tape-recorder out of my coat pocket, he delved into the desk drawer and brought out fistfuls of batteries, 'in case you lose the power'.

By contemporary standards, Mickey was a late starter as a car thief.

Well, they say you always remember your first; well, mine was a Mini. Everybody nicked Minis, all my mates had been at it a while. . . . Usually you went up West for a night out, got pissed and nicked a motor to get home . . . Minis were the easiest—just whack out the little quarter-light and pull this little wire they had instead of a handle and that was it. I was a bit windy at first so I never got too involved, I just watched and got a lift home. I must have been 18 when I did my first one. I say that because I had a licence and was working as a van-driver.

Driving was always a buzz—not going fast, not Stirling Moss or nothing, just being in a car. So till I got me own motor I just used to go for Minis. Well Minis mostly—sometimes Anglias or Poplar (*sic*).

Mickey's enthusiasm rapidly turned to expertise, enhanced by the acquisition of a set of keys.

I bought them from a geezer in the pub. (Laughs.) Yeah, I know it's what you say to the Old Bill, but it's true. I knew this geezer, a wannabee you might call him—always shooting his cuffs and talking big. You know, money, birds, blagging. Nobody takes him seriously, a fucking loser, a joke. Then one day he comes in with a fucking great ring of keys, waving them all over the place. Reckons he can get in almost any motor. We all piss ourselves. So he takes us outside and does nearly every motor in the car park. So I gets him pissed and buys 'em off him for 75 sovs. [£75].

Professional status was instantly acquired.

When the word got out about the keys, I could charge geezers £75 a night and they would borrow them. I give up me job and bought into a stall on the markets with me cousin. Then people would come to me with special orders . . . and I would do 'em myself. But joke was people thought the keys was magic, and a lot of motors I couldn't get into so I had to find other ways.

I just learnt as I went on. I mean if you ask most people if they can get into their motor when they've lost their keys they can do it—coat-hangers, bits of plastic, all that. That's how it was for me, just ordinary common-sense stuff. But I had to be so quick and although I say it myself, it is a question of bottle. Having a nice BMW, and it's sitting all plump and ripe, and I know that I have got a punter with a large pile of notes waiting, then I must be able to go and take it. Don't matter about skill—skill you learn getting in, wiring and away. Honest, anybody can do it. The Old Bill, even them if you forget your keys, they will turn up and do it for you. Difference is the pressure, the buzz is on you to do it under pressure. (Breaks into song.) 'Fuck-ups, I've had a few, but then again too few to mention.'

It was wrong, of course it was, especially when I first started. I would make a mess so the punter could knock me down, damaged goods like. Or I would make too much noise and have to do a runner. To be fair, that never really happened too often. The thing was I got a good name as a thief before I was really good. People think it's harder than it is to do a motor at least they used to before kids started doing motors for radios. See, when I started you did a motor to nick it, no other reason, there weren't that many motors with radios. Some thieves would have radios but for me I was doing it to order—and class motors too—so I never really fucked about with anything in the car.

Once had a Cortina GTI Mark 1 out of Brentwood. I gets on the A13 and hears something moving in the back. Only an Alsatian asleep. Delivered motor, dog, and all, never charged no extra. (Laughs.)

Mickey served two years for car theft and when he came out was forced to reassess his career.

The market all changed. Well yeah, but you change yourself as you get older. I mean, the two stretch I did, it shook me. When I come out I had to get organized—sorted out.

Now this was just about, well I come out in 1976 . . . get a car to order and leave it somewhere quiet or put it down for a couple of weeks and put it out on the day. I was never over-involved. The big successful teams I think did it all themselves. Like I say, there is no trick to it. But sometimes they would ask for something special, might be something quick, or an old builder's van, depending. When I come out, yeah, when I come out, I looked around, and lot of people, not so much friends but acquaintances, had gone down for three or four handfuls (fifteen or twenty years) that I had to think about the future.

Mickey invested his savings in a newsagent's. Later he sold it and opened a video shop in the suburbs. However, it was the opening in 1981 of a travel agency that provided him with a 'proper' commercial base for his thieving.

While I had the paper-shop I was still involved, but not all that. I met this geezer inside who was part of a firm of ringers in Bow, and I did some work with them. The thing with ringing is that there is not the money in pulling the motor. You might get a oner or so, but the ringing, doing the chassis number and reregistering it from the number on a write-off, there is so much to be made there. I fell out with people who were doing it . . . over money, the usual. Again really it's like anything—it's not a difficult thing to do and it takes no time. That's why now it's just boys taking the car and handing it over to a ringer, and if he's got a buyer, then within, what, less than a couple . . . in a day he's laid out a couple of hundred sovs. top and pulled anything, nice few grand.

The video shop was a loser at first but when everybody got videos I was there—even run a delivery service. Loads of pirates, Long John Silver weren't in it. One contact I had could get any film on video. I made a lot of money out of stuff like ET . . . I started doing some work for a contact who sold [cars] direct to the Continent. He was a thief like himself, like used to specialize in top British motors, Jags, Daimlers, all sorts of sports cars. He'd deliver to Germany where his contact was—go over on the ferry himself and fly back. What a target he was . . . nicked him driving one of these lary motors. Got chatting to me when he came out, and we decided to be more businesslike about the whole thing. Cut down on risk—smooth things out.

By the early 1980s Mickey's new partner had renegotiated his relationship with the German importers to accommodate the expanding demand from the Middle East for high-quality European cars. Centres for dealing in stolen cars were established in both East and West Germany. From these depots, modifications were made (e.g. air-conditioning) before being transported to dealers who specialized in Middle Eastern trading, or directly to customers. Mickey initially worked as both thief and exporter, shipping the vehicles out in containers that bore documentation relevant to cheap, normally undesirable vehicles.

Now, doing it this way was sweet but expensive. We would buy old shit-heaps at auction, half a dozen at a time, store 'em away, stash 'em till we needed 'em. Usually old Japanese motors, but 'em for £150, £200. Purloin a Jag and ship it out in a container using an old Datsun's documents . . . Just to be safe we would have the Datsun crushed at the same time. So any come-backs it's 'Sorry it was a Datsun when it left us.' But it was costing us a lot of money and we felt, well, on offer really' cos any come-backs led to us.

The answer was to set up a series of ever-mobile limited companies. These companies would 'own' the vehicles bought from auction and pay Mickey's travel firm, now operating as a shipping agency, to export the goods.

It worked very well for us. We knew what the Germans want, so any top-quality motor we can move. Even Mercs and BMWs, the right models, we just ship 'em out. For a special price I would drive out or let somebody drive a motor over, but that is going to be very expensive. After having it, it gets laid down for a while, ringed, you know engine and chassis number changed, sometimes sprayed but not often.

Then after a while we will drive it out, drop it off, get a train to, say, Frankfurt, away from the depot, and fly back from there. We did that, what, only four times in nine years. It costs loads. The risk, the ringing, the expenses, but for the right motor, say a brand new Jag, they will pay the money. . . . After a while, well, if it come on top then, well how you supposed to explain a Merc when it's supposed to be a Datsun? . . . No, we just stopped ringing. Once you get captured and they look even a little bit close at the chassis and engine, well, they know. Nobody does it perfect, so we cut all that out. Like I say, now it's rare. I suppose that from their point of view they can always get somebody cheaper than us—there are so many people at it.

More recently Mickey and co. have expanded into the market for heavy plant, and road-making equipment.

It came through our German contacts, but we have now got our own and away. Sometimes, again for the right price, we get all the documentation arranged beforehand and the lorry takes it straight to the docks. Heavy plant vehicles are good. Well, mainly it's working at night in out-of-the-way places with plenty of time to work. Usually we got someone there working, say, on the roads who knows the score, knows the vehicle security, the lot. The only problems we come across was when we sold some stuff to a firm of tarmackers and about two years later the gear turns up at an auction in Kent. They couldn't trace it to us, but the site manager who was with us, he was nicked. Since then I won't deal in this country. I just move the stuff quick.

It's contacts in Ireland and we deal direct with them. Security is so sloppy on most sites it's a piece of shit. Say a 'dozer, it's up on a flat bed [lorry] down to wherever docks and away. . . . I will arrange it all, the paper, whatever. But it's like the motors, it's faded right away. I don't often touch motors any more. To be honest, some of the kids around now are better than me, they get in, wire it, and away.

It's a very clean business that has been good to me and my family. . . . I wouldn't get in to anything else, at my age the risk is too—I mean, like too much to lose. The video shop and the travel [agent's] side of things are still going great and I don't need the buzz any more. Apart from that two stretch, the Old Bill have never been near me. To nick me they would have to have a team of about ten on to me for fucking ever, touring the world, names, numbers, accounts. . . . I don't have to rush it now. I can take my time. The younger ones now will put themselves on offer for a penny. There's not the money that you hear about. You can really put yourself on offer for really nothing. . . . So I made mine. It's a pick-and-choose thing. I don't have to go to really graft any more. Fact is I was thinking about doing a book like yours on the motor trade. (Laughs.) No, why bother? It's not worth the candle. Why me anyway? I am just a businessman who stole a few motors when he was a kid.

Mickey and the Fat Boys are bonded by enterprise. They make money both inside and outside the law, and they are all, according to the view from either side of the shop window, successful. For them economic life is fundamental, defining their very existence in a way that is mirrored in both oak-panelled boardrooms and the darkest alcoves of our inner cities. In their lives there is room for pleasure, humour, and companionship. That they are proud of their achievements and wish for a better life for their children, that there is video evidence of Fat Stan crying at his son's wedding, should not suggest a crude set of parallels between workers in the legitimate and illegitimate economies. They may feed at the same trough and experience many of the same highs and lows, but slag off the Fat Boys or refuse to pay your bill and Peter will probably shoot you. It is to that dark chamber of retribution, rather than to legislative justice, that serious criminals turn to unleash forces of both a business and a personal nature.

5

Mutant Enterprise: Kenny's Story

Kenny lives in a nice street, and as far as he knows, his neighbours are nice people. He bought his bungalow fifteen years ago before the motorway came, linking a semi-comatose retirement village to the pin-striped portals of the City. The ensuing commuter hell pushed up house prices, but not before Kenny had purchased the small parcel of land that backed on to his garden.

When the family saloons start to edge their way out of the close to join the morning's traffic jam, Kenny is waking up his children and preparing breakfast. Kenny has four children, a 28-year-old from his first marriage, and two boys and a girl aged 5, 7, and 9, who attend local schools. His wife works in an estate agent's office about ten miles away, and after she has left the house in her neat 2-year-old hatchback, it is up to Kenny to perform the school run. The double garage is the most recent of numerous extensions to the bungalow which have transformed the original 1950s structure into a suburban fortress. A new kitchen-diner overlooks the pond where koi carp drift, and a Georgian-style games-room was built on to the side of the house when one of Kenny's offspring began to show an interest in table tennis. A large rectangular extension juts threateningly from the roof, the sills of the picture windows guarded by soft toys. After dropping the kids off in a four-wheel-drive Jeep and exchanging pleasantries at the school gate, Kenny goes to work.

Kenny is a businessman. He owns a video hire shop, and has a share in a used-car business. He also deals in amphetamines and cocaine. Until five years ago he regularly imported pornography into the country, and his girlfriend is currently in prison for her part in a major conspiracy involving forged foreign currency. Kenny is typical of an entrepreneurial mutant that has evolved from the economic and ideological foundations of late twentieth-century British enterprise culture. He is virtually indistinct from the undermanagers, plumbers, and insurance salesmen with whom he shares the stone-clad certainties of a suburban cul-de-sac, hewn from the remnants of post-industrial society. He wears shell-suit trousers and a close-fitting polo shirt as he wheels the weekly shopping around the hypermart, is on first-name terms with the proprietor of his local Thai restaurant, and believes that rapists should be raped. He oozes a sense of well-being that can only be achieved by successfully engaging with the market-place at a consistently high level over a period of many years.

LITTLE ACORNS

Kenny emerged from an inner-city neighbourhood firm in the early 1970s. His credentials at that time appear to amount to little more than a willingness to work and a desire to make money. There is no hint of violence in his biography, and his reputation, as a young man was that of a shrewd wheeler-dealer. As an ex-colleague of Kenny's explained,

As long as I could remember you could always go to him and get him to move whatever. A container-load of engine parts, a lorry-load of suits, he was always able to help out. . . . Even as a kid he was stone-cold reliable, sensible with prices and that, could always move stuff that others would like hum and ha over.

It is possible to trace Kenny's career back over more than two decades, and the characteristic most consistently identified was his integrity. I found nobody who had been ripped off or conned by Kenny. He was, as his cousin Charlie, who owns a string of garages, explained, 'a real pleasure to do business with'. His initial success appears to be related to his willingness to purchase whole loads from thieves. For by buying wholesale, and selling retail, he was able both to maximize his profits and to increase his cultural collateral within an environment that places a high premium upon entrepreneurial competence.

Kenny's career began when, as a fringe member of a well-established neighbourhood firm, he sold stolen motor-scooter parts and accessories to chrome-hungry mods. Charlie told me:

He was always better at the selling than the rest of us. But because it was like more often than not you was nicking from the same ones you was selling to, sometimes it come on top and there could be a ruck. That wasn't him. Not that he would be on his toes, but he was never what you might call a hard case. But he could sell anything, always turn a profit and not upset people. . . . They all liked Kenny, and even now people from when we was kids will go to him, and if he can't do something then he will put them into somebody who can.

Kenny married at 17, was a father at 19, and served his first prison sentence at 21. To welfarists and rearmers of moral economies alike, such a stark chronology may reaffirm well-established images of alienation, deprivation, and delinquent inbreeding. However, the details that fill the gaps between these biographical lines belie such assertions, and a life of some complexity is revealed; a life that is sustained by the intensity and vitality of deviant action.

When Kenny married Susan she was several months pregnant, but miscarried within weeks of moving into their new home, the back bedroom of Susan's grandmother's house. Within the year the house was subject to a compulsory purchase order and the newly-weds were rehoused in a brand new three-bedroomed council house. At the age of 18 Kenny had the capacity to store complete consignments of stolen goods. Moving into three bedrooms, a lounge, and a lock-up garage may not seem like an obvious business opportunity, but soon the advantage of the neighbourhood having its very own 'slaughter' soon became apparent, and the money, along with the suits, meat, carpets, televisions, and the rest, all came rolling in. No more tedious, hazardous excursions to Essex or Kent in the early hours, to be met at the end of a dark track by strangers in the shadows of rat-infested barns and long-redundant rolling-stock. Kenny's family home became a community resource. A twenty-four-hour neighbourhood centre, without a social worker or a local authority grant in sight, run by a teenager, and driven by enterprise over a decade before the term was invented.

When he was arrested it was for a crime as mundane and unspectacular as the man himself. Kenny, cousin Charlie, and an older man who was a friend of the family were delivering a lorry-load of tinned corned beef to a warehouse owned by a now defunct chain of local grocers. The tins were the remainder of a load stolen from the docks, and Kenny was committed to purchase the entire consignment. Local people, cafés, and businesses rapidly snapped up bargains by the case-load, and Kenny quickly made a connection with the owner of the chain of grocers whose sell-by date was even more imminent than that of the corned beef. The deal included delivery—not an unusual arrangement for large orders—and consisted of the remainder of the load. Charlie relates:

We lent a lorry off some mate of Kenny's and it wouldn't start at the lights. Old Bill comes along and we just sit there trying to get it started. When they look in the back, we just hold up our hands. Then when they give his drum a spin and get into the lock-ups they can't believe the result they got. There's bits of this and a carton of that, stuff that got left over . . . just bits. Eighteen months'—worth, only three months a slice for me and the other geezer.

Kenny's eighteen-month sentence was his first brush with the criminal justice system, and without the benefit of conditioning by approved schools and borstals it must have been a chastening experience. Indeed this was his last taste of prison for fifteen years.

On his release Kenny bought an old van and converted it into a mobile café. The van's regular pitch was on wasteland next to one of the south-east's major freight depots, where lorries from all over Europe would converge. Working long shifts, Kenny, his family, and their associates provided lorry-drivers with hot tea, bacon sandwiches, and the best prices for any surplus that might seep from bloated cargoes. Kenny started by buying odd cartons that were superfluous to the consignment's paperwork, and rapidly progressed to purchasing part-loads and loads. This escalation of his activities was achieved by forming alliances with clerical and loading staff working in two of the major shipping companies inside the depot. Clerical staff would sift shipping manifests of goods awaiting delivery and pass the details of likely targets to Charlie, who now takes up the story:

It would depend really what it was. A lot of stuff like, it would always come in a small parcel and he could go to work with it night or day. Top-of-the-range clothes, reams of cloth, electric. It's the sort of gear you can get a buyer without setting it up beforehand. But he made a point of letting them know, and setting it up with the paper and the loaders and everybody treating it serious. If they didn't, if it was just 'Oh it will do for him', and out of the blue some driver turns up with a load of old toot nobody going to buy, then they still want paying. That's the point, they all wanted paying top to bottom, but if you let that occur then the money's all tied up with total shit.

Kenny would place his order with his shipping company contacts, who would then ensure that the relevant contacts with lorry—drivers were made. These drivers would then stop off for sustenance at Kenny's van, parking out of the glare of the terminal's floodlights, just backstage of the lard-drenched ambience of the most profitable greasy spoon in town.

The goods were then transferred to an appropriate van or lorry, and taken either to waiting customers or to holding accommodation. Inside the terminal, the consignment would be checked against the relevant paperwork and confirmed as complete. By the time the consignment had reached its final destination and the anomalies discovered, the stolen goods had been wholesaled, retailed, and made indistinct from goods of more legitimate origins.

With the van as a base, Kenny developed over the next seven years an elaborate network of contacts that extended across the country. Drivers with 'spare' loads and 'spare' keys, companies with surplus goods following a fire, thieves, burglars, and jump-up men would seek out Kenny. Drop-off and change-over points were established, and warehouses, lock-up garages, and 'slaughters' were set up by Kenny in order to cope with his blossoming trade.

Occasionally there would be a mishap, an arrest, prison. However, these were in every way isolated incidents, relating to individual acts of skulduggery. For with police action confining itself to the acts of theft, the enabling networks that sustain larceny are neither identified nor given significance. Indeed the loose coalitions that whirled around Kenny's mobile greasy spoon, particularly when observed through a legal lens, present such an amorphous image of unstructured criminality as to make their detection and legal obliteration little more than a crime squad officer's wet dream.

Even those regularly making money from the greasy spoon's illegal enterprise were limited to their individual scripts. Only a part of the structural arrangements of Kenny's business could be comprehended—a snapshot portraying a particular time and place. Dennis worked for three years as a shipping clerk inside the freight terminal.

I got to know him through my sister, who knew his mum from the old leatherworks. We used to move the paperwork through after bits of the load had gone missing . . . just put it through as complete. That's all I ever did, nothing really. We would meet up of a Friday for a drink and I got paid, what £20, £30, whatever it was. . . . I don't know what I was earning at the time, but it was probably no more than twenty or thirty quid [a

week].... It depended on what was going on at the time, but at one time there was three
or four on the [loading] bank—me, and the office was always changing, and it was shifts,
so it depended who was about. But me and another bloke was regular. What, five or six
[were involved]. Not every week but most weeks we probably all got paid something
from him.

Dennis's awareness of the scale of Kenny's enterprise was limited to his own
experience, which only involved, the falsification of shipping documents and the
consequent receipt of payment. Dennis was sacked for running highly profitable
Sunday afternoon film shows inside the warehouse featuring imported porno-
graphic films recently 'confiscated' by Customs officials.

Charlie, however, had a more comprehensive view of Kenny's business.

Anybody with a lock-up who wanted to earn could just give us the keys and forget about
it. We had lock-ups all over. We got people to front up on warehouses and we put gear
in them. There was rented vans coming and going. When I look back we did so much
and Kenny was at the middle. ... He was the youngest, but he was trusted, and he had
a good eye for a deal. People come to him, they still do. As a buyer and a seller he is
the best. Not a bully, not somebody who goes into a deal to slaughter people.

It is impossible to estimate how much money Kenny was earning at this time,
but it certainly did not manifest itself in a sumptuous life-style. His family home
remained a three-bedroomed council house, and his car a second-hand Ford.
Most of the money was kept circulating in a market that frequently made sudden
demands upon his financial resources. There were also constant demands upon
Kenny's time and energy. He was always working: on the telephone, loading
and unloading, 3 a.m. meetings in lay-bys, business over a fried breakfast, over
lager at lunch-time and more lager in the evening. People were paid off and
others courted for payment. Then it all stopped.

FRY UP, BURN OUT

Kenny was drinking heavily, and his health was rapidly deteriorating. By his late
twenties he had lost not only most of his hair, but also his wife and child, of
whom he had seen very little as his work increasingly kept him away from
home. Two of those closest to Kenny's business were convicted of grievous
bodily harm following a fracas in a pub, and he fell into dispute with Charlie.
The precise nature of the dispute is unclear as Charlie was unwilling to discuss
it. However, after I talked to several contemporaries of both men, and to Charlie's
wife, it became apparent that Kenny's drinking had affected his judgement and
a consignment of meat had been purchased from a group of thieves with a
reputation for both violence and sharp practice.

Kenny had paid for the goods without checking the contents of the lorry, and
it was only when he attempted to sell them that it was discovered that the lorry's

refrigeration unit had been turned off for a considerable period of time, rendering the load worthless. Kenny passed the loss off as an unfortunate consequence of doing business with thieves, while Charlie, after remonstrating with his younger cousin, confronted the men and demanded repayment. He was hospitalized for a month, and soon after Kenny was rushed to hospital with a perforated ulcer.

The next few years are rather difficult to map out in terms of Kenny's criminal career. For most of this period he continued to drink heavily, and consequently remained in poor health. He became estranged from most of his family, and as his general level of competency declined, accomplices and business associates moved on. In an effort to revive his fortunes, Kenny moved his mobile café to a twenty-four-hour lorry park where he continued to buy stolen goods. However, he could no longer sustain the pace, and the scale of his operation was now much smaller, piecemeal and unpredictable. Kenny was now only offered the odd carton or item. He no longer had either the contacts or the business acumen to deal with whole loads. By the age of 30 he was a drunk working seven days a week, serving tea and fried bacon to lorry-drivers. He developed the habit of buying cheap bottles of duty-free whisky from drivers returning from trips abroad, consuming them while working, and sleeping off the effects in the van.

Kenny met Wendy just a few weeks before he was arrested for possession of stolen goods, which Charlie mockingly explained amounted to '500 ladies' handbags and cardboard briefcases'. When the police searched his home and lock-up they discovered the flotsam and jetsam of over ten years' buying and selling stolen goods. When he came out of prison just over a year later, he married Wendy, moved into her flat, sold the van, and vowed never to drink again. He also invested his meagre savings in a consignment of contraband tobacco, and within a year Kenny and Wendy were bungalow-bound.

ROLLING HIS OWN

Tobacco-smuggling became extremely important to criminal entrepreneurs during the late 1970s and early to mid-1980s. Lorry-drivers travelling on the Continent were bringing back small amounts of rolling-tobacco for their own consumption. The tobacco had been imported from Britain and could be bought cheaply in Holland or Belgium and smuggled back into the country without paying tax. A cottage industry soon developed and it was not long before entrepreneurs were making major investments. False compartments were built, trailers hired, and drivers paid on average £200 per trip. Kenny still had a few contacts in the transport and haulage industry, and he quickly re-established the cultural collateral that he had acquired before he started drinking.

Kenny was reconciled with Charlie, who rapidly became crucial to the enterprise, taking particular responsibility for hiring trailers and seeking out legitimate consignments in the Low Countries as a cover for the smuggling operation. Kenny was totally removed from the day-to-day running of the smuggling enterprise, concentrating his efforts upon a used-car business he had established close to his new home.

Tobacco-smuggling opened up possibilities for the importation of more profitable commodities, and several operatives experimented with importing hashish from the Continent, often using the same methodology that had proved successful with tobacco. However, Charlie's brother in-law and a business partner travelled further afield and bought a large quantity of hash from the Moroccan police, who promptly arrested them at the border, confiscated the dope, and negotiated a hefty bribe. Such tales were not uncommon at this time as middle-aged working-class criminals, usually with minimal knowledge either of the culture of recreational drug use or of the commerce that accompanied it, attempted to exploit this new market.

By the mid-1970s there was a discernible shift amongst a generation of the more successful armed robbers as they exploited the cultural and monetary capital that they had acquired as a result of their professional activities, in order to engage with the drug market. While this shift has been well documented, there is a tendency to underestimate the extent to which a whole range of entrepreneurs were made aware of the commercial possibilities proffered by the new market for recreational drugs. Criminal and non-criminal entrepreneurial types were not driven to drug-dealing purely by ageing, alterations to some mythic criminal subculture, the success of the police in dealing with serious crime, or improvements in commercial security. For although these developments were important, they were not crucial for the expansion of recreational drug markets. The 'big bang' was created by demand, and commercially competent individuals, particularly those with access to transport and storage facilities, were as well equipped as any to engage with the market.

However, this market was not geographically or culturally parochial, and many individuals who had been weaned on the locally orientated criminal entrepreneurship that typified traditional British crime backed away from this prime money-making opportunity. Territoriality was the main stumbling-block. 'Going on somebody else's manor' was problematic enough; doing business with foreigners beyond the pale. The usual rationale for this abstinence was a traditional (and therefore superior) moral stance. Drugs *per se* were wrong, alien, and the prerogative of hippies and foreigners. Even users were quick to establish the parameters of their involvement. The more unimaginative of the serious-crime community, with the enthusiastic co-operation of the mass media, proceeded to construct a golden-age scenario for British crime that evoked a post-war era of hard but fair principled rogues. These individuals played by the rules, never hurt civilians, were respected members of the community, and would under no circumstances deal in drugs. Given that most of the key players in this major historical reconstruction were either dead or serving long prison sentences, it was relatively easy to ignore the involvement of these almost mythic characters in the admittedly low-key drug trade of their era.

PREVIOUS CONVICTIONS

The construction of golden-age scenarios is as important to the way crime is perceived in contemporary society as it is to our understanding of traditional and post-traditional social control. By resorting to golden-age rhetoric, traditional serious-crime personnel can cloak not only their own entrepreneurial timidity but also the parasitical heart of serious criminal enterprise. These dinosaurs of crime employ a rhetoric that, like their clothes and haircuts, pre-date 1963. They can be easily identified by their fish-eyed stare and pre-Open University lag-speak. The shine on the suit is a reflection of aged worsted rather than ten-ounce mohair. Albert missed the boat.

You could trust people more. And if you did have a fight it was none of this with shooters and that. You had a stand-up and that was that. . . . Razors? It was what you did. Not saying it was right but there was times when razors was used on people, I will admit that. But it was only on others the same, who was going to do the same to you. . . . And they looked after people—old people and that. Now they just don't worry about nothing, no old people, nothing like that.

I asked about drugs—was there much of that?

Nothing, no. It was the blacks who come it with all that. I never even knew about it till they started doing all that. Then it was all the mugging and that, 'cos they get addicted with the needles and that. In my day it was a case of, really, I suppose, just being a thief. You read about the drugs and that . . . and on the telly with the pop stars and then the hippies, but the likes of us you never touch, I mean you never even knew about it. . . . Them that do just top them. I mean they give them to kids like sweets now. In my day that could never have been the case. We would have dealt with that before it got out of hand. We would never have put up, with it. . . . It was safer than now. Now, with the mugging and the drugs and that, it's just not safe for no one. . . . I just come in [to the pub] and have a drink, a bet, and home.

Albert is no geriatric, he can be no more than 55 years old. His last prison sentence was in the early 1970s, when he was involved in a long-standing family feud that resulted in the shooting of a man who was also a business rival. By the time he had served his sentence, the market-place had altered to the extent that he could no longer participate. Eight years is a long time in crime, and Albert found that his economic viability had deteriorated along with his health. A heart defect was diagnosed in prison, and he now lives with his wife, a hospital cleaner, in a two-bedroomed maisonette.

While Albert lives on his invalidity pension, Kenny continues to live on his wits. The two men are almost contemporaries, their backgrounds virtually identical, yet they are divided by their ability and willingness to adapt and engage with the market-place. For Albert the new market is a frightening and alien place, devoid of those traditions of community that are mourned by most ageing populations. The violence, greed, and associated hardship and deprivation of the past have become sanctified relics of an era of hard men and essentially communal deviation. For Kenny, however, drugs are just another commodity to be bought and sold, another chance to make money. Kenny has never been a team player or harboured communal aspirations. As a leading architect of the enterprise culture once explained, 'There is no such thing as society, only individuals and families.' Kenny might add 'and buyers and sellers'.

GOING INTO EUROPE

Kenny moved out of tobacco when a business associate of his was exposed by a tabloid newspaper as a major smuggler. For Kenny pulling out was hardly a wrench as the Customs authorities had already achieved some successes, including the arrest and seizure of some loads he had financed. Whenever possible Kenny used self-employed lorry-drivers who either owned or hired their own units. For experienced drivers with good connections in shipping and haulage companies, this was a viable arrangement. It was also good for Kenny as it meant that the tobacco would be assimilated with other goods by the time they entered the country. Further, it was advantageous to hire the trailers, so that in the event of any contraband being discovered the trailer would be confiscated but not the unit, and the hire company could be left to negotiate with HM Customs. The driver would normally receive a fine. On the few occasions that drivers received custodial sentences, Kenny made a donation to the family's household bills via a third party, usually Charlie.

For a time Kenny, with the connivance of his suppliers in Holland, and usually without the driver's knowledge, had mixed pornography with his loads. His buyer in London was a friend from the old neighbourhood who ran a sex shop. When the site on which the shop was situated was sold to developers, the porn dealer became an estate agent.

The shift to importing dope was as easy as it was logical. However, the arrest and conviction of a number of ex-colleagues who had invested in cannabis importation did make Kenny rather more circumspect, and his subsequent caution was in marked contrast to his early days of frantic wheeling and dealing. He became the silent partner in a freight forwarding company which he set up with two associates with wholly legitimate business backgrounds.

Kenny sells wholesale, and his buyers are not difficult to find, emanating almost exclusively from the entrepreneurial maelstrom that had forged his own career. Kenny deals exclusively with other white middle-aged men, for it is they who dominate the importation and wholesale marketing of amphetamine-based recreational drugs. Within this market violence is a comparative rarity, as demand exceeds supply, and suppliers engage with a market-place largely devoid of the volatile gangsterdom that is often characteristic of street markets.

Kenny moved into amphetamines somewhere between 1984 and 1986. He continued to purchase mainly from Holland and Belgium, and occasionally from Germany. By the time ecstasy became the drug of choice for Britain's youth in the early 1990s, Kenny had established himself as a major importer and wholesaler. Lorries would pass through Customs and unload at one of a number of warehouses around the south-east of England. Buyers were expected to pick up consignments at these locations, and requests to deliver goods were normally turned down. By the late 1980s he was also making occasional sorties into the cocaine market as part of a consortium which, due to the prohibitive cost of white-powder importation, would collaborate to invest in what some close associates of Kenny felt was an unnecessarily risky business. As Charlie says,

It goes against the grain, all this [drugs], but when it was the dope and the speed and that, it was only like, well, the kids was just doing what they all do and you couldn't see no harm really. But with the powder, a lot of people when they knew what it was they never wanted to know. I was out of it. We done very well over the years, and there is no doubt that he [Kenny] has got a brain this big. But I had enough. I was at the point that I wanted to take life a little bit gentler. We had a good run and I never wanted to spoil it.

FACTORY LIFE

Charlie retired in 1992 following two years of chaos. Kenny had no control over the make-up of the consortium that imported cocaine, and he found himself collaborating with men of violence. The seizure of a multimillion pound consignment of cocaine in 1990 was hailed as a significant victory for the police and Customs authorities. However, while the media's attention was focused upon the prominent names, who subsequently received hefty sentences, less well-known investors were merely bankrupted. Several men disappeared abroad in the fall-out of the seizure, and a close friend of Kenny's eldest son had the door of his flat blasted by a shotgun, as some of the more malevolent investors attempted to claim traditional recompense.

Kenny sold his apartment in Spain at a loss, and put more effort into his used-car business in an attempt to accrue some hard cash. By early 1992 his financial situation became critical when an armed robber who had escaped from prison set up an amphetamine sulphate factory next to the old neighbourhood. Kenny's customers and associates were all rooted in the neighbourhood where he had started his business career some thirty years ago, and the establishment of the sulphate factory obliterated Kenny's importation speciality, for the robber had an awesome reputation for violence, to the extent that no blood was spilt during his period establishment of market dominance. Amateurs and freelancers had whittled away at his profits from ecstasy, and drivers were becoming as increasingly aware of the commercial viability of their labour as they had a decade earlier when smuggling tobacco.

Kenny spent more and more time in the old neighbourhood, seeking out deals and reaffirming relationships that had first been established within the context of a market that was cruder yet, from the perspective of many participants, more agreeable than its current manifestation. Colin, an ex-thief now in his mid-fifties, talks about villainy during the 1960s in the same way that ageing football fans speak of players of that era.

Characters they were then . . . the way they dressed and handled themselves you knew, everyone knew, who they was. Villains then would dress the part, immaculate, and if you were around them you had to dress the same. I suppose what I am saying is they carried themselves, how should I say, like people should.

However, the bazaar-like atmosphere of the neighbourhood pubs, clubs, and other crucial trading locations remained the same.

NOBLE ARTS AND LOW BLOWS

By one o'clock the conference suite–dining-room of the Queens is packed. Informal Sunday lunch-time boxing bouts are a long-established ritual in this barnlike pub. Situated in the no man's land between the multi-cultural inner city and the stone-clad laager of semi-detached escapees, the Queens offers a leisure experience that is *Blade Runner* out of *Passport to Pimlico*. Plastic wooden beams run the breadth of the hall, and real ale at unreal prices is delivered via a reproduction hand-pump. The walls are chrome and black plastic, a reminder that the Palm Springs Disco disgorged its last customer less than twelve hours ago. Pink and grey prints of twenties flappers and Brylcreemed men in evening suits and spats are an indication of the nightspots previous incarnation as Gatsby's.

Most of the clientele drink lager straight from the bottle as they stand waiting for the fights to begin. Of the crowd of 250, only about a dozen are women. The bulk of the audience are men in their late twenties and early thirties, with heads shaved at the side and a range of tattoos. This is an affluent audience, the car park full of late registration hot hatchbacks, and 3-year-old BMWs. The atmosphere in the hall is disconcertingly sober, restrained laughter with lashings of wall-eyed indifference being the order of the day. The tension is of the kind experienced in an Indian restaurant two hours after closing-time, as the clientele becomes more dubious by the minute and the Pils starts to seep through to the testosterone.

Kenny has driven to the pub in his Jeep, and though no boxing fan, has forsaken his son's Sunday morning football team to make this important journey. Before the bouts commence Kenny spends his time glad-handing. This is a crucial meeting-place for businessmen, villains, and cardboard gangsters alike; a place to be seen, where the symbolic importance of the violence about to be served up outweighs its shortcomings in terms of either art or craft. For in the audience there are also wild-eyed punters with blood in their eyes who have come to scream for lashings of gore. Whether this occurs in or out of the ring is irrelevant, for as the first fight finishes within thirty seconds of round one the two sets of supporters commence combat with a lack of the guile that the donning of gloves and ringing of bells had at least suggested. The official bout comprised two men dressed in tracksuit bottoms swinging their arms furiously until one fell down exhausted. The lorry-driver's shoulders and publican's stomach of the winner heaved as he left the ring, the loser doused his head with a can of lager, the spectators concluded their own bout, and Kenny got back to business.

Business for Kenny means making himself known and pressing the flesh. These crop-haired men are the generation of entrepreneurs that he now has to deal with in order to reinstate his claim on the ecstasy market. They represent an urban élite which controls access to club sales and street outlets, and as a consequence are that much closer to the violence that accompanies the drugs business when dealers get near users and other dealers. Their potential for violence is overt, worn around their necks like medallions of pure snide gold, obvious, reckless, and in intimidatory bad taste. Kenny is clearly uncomfortable with this retrograde, but necessary, new phase of his career, but his reputation is such that nobody shuns this unprepossessing middle-aged man.

The respect that he receives is manifested in polite conversation, or, in an environment that is dominated by a large advertisement for cock and hen nights above a boxing-ring now containing two Sikhs thumping each other to the delight of the crop-haired audience, what passes for polite conversation. This consists of coded references to business, trade, and most importantly to a generic competence in all matters monetary and violent. A mere presence at such gatherings, and the ability of actors to assume an essentially élitist demeanour apart from the blood, snot, and gore of the punters at the ringside, is a crucial factor in the process of invention and reinvention that enables actors to engage with the market-place as it mutates from wholesale to retail zones of enacted commerce. However, there is a limit to how often Kenny can reinvent himself. Violence has always been an anathema to his practice, which is based upon buying and selling. Now in his late forties, 2 stone over weight, and with the posture of a clerk, he knows that the assumption of menace is hardly feasible. A new generation has taken over responsibility for aspects of the market that lay close to those zones of commercial activity struck by periodic and haphazard resort to the folk memories of family feuds, by personal slights or the raw sensuality of wanton savagery. Here lurks chaos, poverty, and myriad forms of personal oblivion.

As traditional employment and associated labour support mechanisms have drained away, so communal economic strategies and their accompanying rhetorics, both legitimate and illegitimate, have become increasingly inappropriate. This is the point where the rationality of the market-place finds its credit limit, and this is the place Kenny has been trying to avoid all his adult life. By the time the final bout commenced, Kenny was looking exhausted. He had made his presence known, and done his best to establish himself, but his pitch was limited. Devoid of either the campaign scars or ostentatious wealth that denotes victory, and with a demeanour and gait more appropriate to the carvery upstairs, Kenny looks like somebody's dad out for a few lagers while the roast beef and Bisto coagulate at home.

In the ring an immaculately coiffured surfer in lycra shorts is back-pedalling skilfully to avoid the onslaught of a short, squat opponent with densely compacted muscle and a mauve tattoo of a parachute on his left shoulder. The surfer shrouded his desperation with bodybuilders poses in between flurries, and the noise in the hall reaches deafening levels of fury and hilarity. At ringside a young woman whose dark roots match her leather trousers, shook her yellow mane furiously as she exhorted her favourite to 'put him in the fucking grinder'. Most of the surfer's elegant jabs bounce harmlessly from the top of the ex-para's thinning pate, and once cornered the bodybuilder succumbs to the grinder, and sinks slowly to the canvas under a barrage of body punches.

There is breaking glass over by the stacked speakers, and a woman screams ringside as half a dozen bodybuilders enter the ring. The victor shows no emotion as his friends and family begin to celebrate, and an elderly man in an ancient beige cardigan climbs through the ropes and proceeds to berate the surfer, who with the assistance of his heavily muscled entourage and a bottle of Evian water is slowly returning to his feet.

The last bout is over, and Kenny has worked as hard as any of the fighters to impress a sceptical audience. However, the deterioration in his viability as a top-class operative was matched by his physical decline and within two months he was rushed to hospital suffering from ulcers.

ABLE TO DABBLE

For several years Kenny had maintained a clandestine relationship with a woman he had first met in Spain while he was decorating the family's holiday apartment. Soon after his release from hospital, the woman, who owned a small shop in Spain but lived on the south coast of England, was arrested for her part in a massive counterfeiting fraud involving foreign currency. The police operation had uncovered a wide range of criminal activity, in which Kenny had played a peripheral part, and when he emerged from hospital he was convinced that he too would be arrested, and worse still that his wife would find out about the affair. Charlie, too, is concerned:

He's got to think about what he wants—what he can do and what he can't do. He is somebody who will always make a living, and not working for somebody else, but in a little business or something of his own. Like with the video shop, it's a lovely little thing he's got there, and he would still be able to dabble how he liked with whatever come up. . . . He's older now and it's not like when we was kids.

There's more money and more fucking aggravation, and it's killing him. When we go out tonight you watch him—he's in a dream, he's gone like an old man, don't talk or laugh. He wants to leave all that heavy business well alone. Look what happened with that sort he was seeing. Now I am not going to sit here and slag the man off over it. What he does is his business. But instead of finding himself a little sort and having a nice time, he goes and tows behind somebody like her, and starts going into bits of deals with her. He don't need it, but he loves doing deals. I know what he is like, and look at the state it has got him in. He is a sick man.

By late 1992 Kenny had established himself as a wholesaler of ecstasy. He bought directly from a factory that imported the liquid drug from Holland and converted it into tablet form. However, this venture was short-lived, as the factory entered a form of receivership quite common in the mutant enterprise zone and its owners were imprisoned for conspiracy to smuggle and supply the drug.

There is no neat ending to Kenny's story. He still takes the kids to school, and makes a living from the video store, the used-car business, and whatever deals he can instigate. He is not a rich man, but his children are unlikely to go short of shell suits. Neither is he violent, but he is on good dealing terms with a number of men who are extremely violent. He is a man of exceptionally modern morals, a businessman who loves his car, his family, and large bundles of used currency. But above all else he loves to trade.

At the annual award night of Kenny's son's football team, Charlie told Kenny that I was interested in crime and that I was paid to teach courses on the subject at a university. Kenny seized the opportunity to proffer his own views on law and order:

I wish you could tell me about it then. Nobody has any respect. Everybody knows you make a living whatever way you have to. But by the time kids get to school they just do what they like. The rapes and that . . . there's no stopping people from doing what they like. There's clamp-down coming, and I'll tell you, and I mean this, I'll be there when the time comes. Something's got to be done. Its getting out of hand.

A brief discussion of the various favoured punishments for sex criminals followed, before Kenny, sensing a deal on a 'sweet top-of-the-range Subaru', withdrew to talk business with another proud father. The potential buyer was his accountant.

6

Youth Opportunities: The People's Game

By the time we came out of the heaving club he had been unconscious for two or three minutes. Steam rose gently from the young man's torso as he lay motionless on the cold night pavement, and although it was impossible to ascertain precisely what had happened, the fact that he had kicked Taff was all we needed to know. Taff and Viv had merely done their job, which in this case meant battering the young man and propelling him down the steps of what had once been a cinema, to rest bloodlessly amongst the fast-food packets, cigarette-ends, and puddles of indeterminate liquids that constitute the detritus of just another Saturday night.

Taff and Viv were nowhere in sight when the police arrived. They were inside the club in a room at the back of the main bar drinking Perrier water when the police spoke to the two official bouncers in big suits, with big necks and bow-ties, who had seen nothing. They had seen nothing of the youth's attempt to re-enter the club with a packet of fish and chips from the local take-away, and they had little trouble convincing the two PCs, one with a decoration on his uniform, that it was just a scuffle between local youths, routine stuff and nothing to do with the rave night at the club. 'Good as gold, must be the drugs that keep them quiet.' They laughed.

VIV Strange to have to give somebody a dig. No drink see, just the Es and speed, here for a good night.

TAFF And it's down to us to make sure they have a good time.

VIV They don't even come on the pull, most of them, so they don't have rows about who's going with who. So it's on the door that's where the work is. Make sure you don't get drunks, beer monsters, going to naus it all up.

TAFF Then its 'Sorry lads—just a kids' night.' You let the suits do it first 'cos its their number. 'No beer here—just a kids' night—try down the road—half-price tonight. There's a cab over there.'

VIV We just sort of lurk a bit and gradually join in the talk. And it works 'cos we don't wear monkey suits, and as they keep coming and we join in they know it's getting more serious. If a bouncer goes down then they all want to get a kick in. If there's a bunch for a night out, say twenty or forty, and they're on a coach, if there's a ruck they all want to say they give the bouncer one.

TAFF That cunt was just out of his face. Once he had a pop, he had to go.

VIV He'd been inside, got sorted, been dancing for hours. What's he want fish and fucking chips for?

TAFF He was gonna be a problem inside so we chatted away. Bottom line on this is 'You ain't coming back in with them [fish and chips]'. He got silly.
VIV We fucking hit him, plain and simple. Wankers like him bad for business.

The proprietors of the club had been running raves for several months using their regular security staff, but problems had developed that had brought the club to the attention of the police and local media. Inside it was just another youth venue, playing popular dance music to locals who had picked up enough clues from the house and acid house myth to dress baggy and perform mental under the bought-in lights. The local newspaper reports concerning fights and routine drug-dealing were supplemented by feature articles on drugs and youth culture, and at that point Gary's firm was invited to provide an additional security system.

A GAME OF TWO HALVES

Gary and Eric made names for themselves in the early 1980s as local neighbourhood men of violence. They were prominent members of an infamous group of football hooligans, and along with so many other young people growing up in the 1980s, enterprise culture proved seductive. They were, in the words of playwright Al Hunter, '1980s Thatcher's eagles', not unknowing dupes of rightwing dogma but young people growing up in a society in which few traditional occupational options remained. By the end of that decade they had matured along with the myth of enterprise culture. Some had family commitments, and the police were paying increasing attention to an activity that had been put under the spotlight by a government intent on seeking out successes for their ailing law and order manifesto.[1]

When rave culture marked an explicit shift from overt violence to a more mellow casual style, a marginal semi-deviant market was created that required its own structures and control mechanisms. Raves' emergent entrepreneurs required some way of policing these highly lucrative events, and looked to the old neighbourhoods for the necessary muscle. In many cases the most obvious candidates were those with ready-made reputations forged as members of hooligan firms.[2]

Gary *et al.* were ready and willing. Some events made token gestures towards extracting drugs from a culture founded upon drug use, and when they were instructed to search the arriving punters and confiscate drugs, they moved into the business themselves. Initially they were paid off by dealers who were granted entrance to the event and were able to operate a monopoly. Later they merely confiscated everybody's drugs and set up dealerships themselves. There was seldom any trouble at these events, for Gary's firm were now protecting profits, not merely reputations. Their ferocity remained a crucial asset of their enterprise, and when the police became involved they were dealt with as individuals, rather than as members of a criminal conspiracy that was rapidly expanding into the importation of amphetamines and was claiming a crucial slice of various youth-orientated counterfeiting operations.

Their operation expanded naturally with the legitimization of the rave market. Every provincial town soon had its own 'rave nights', and as club and disco owners cashed in, they inherited the control strategies of the bootleg entrepreneurs, and the ex-hooligan firms were recruited to provide a visceral, informal back-up to the local bodybuilders and farmboys who normally blocked out the light.

Having experimented with a number of variations on the theme of cutting out the middle man, by 1992 Gary and Eric's firm was vigorously enforcing the no-drugs policy, after licensing an associate to deal from a local pub. Anyone going into the club had to consume the drug first, and if they required topping up the firm had the monopoly inside. Driving home in Taff's rented estate car Viv told him that the local dealer whom they supply and license had told him about a new club starting up nearby, and that he would keep them informed of any new marketing opportunities. During the night I had seen no money or drugs changing hands until Viv started snorting cocaine as we came off the motorway. He was playing football later that morning and wanted to be sharp. Taff explained that their method was the best way to police the situation:

TAFF They want the stuff, it's going in the place anyway, so all you can do is make it right for the kids who want to do it in peace.
D.H. And make a few bob?
VIV Fucking right I do.

Gary and Eric gradually distanced themselves from the day-to-day muscle work and concentrated on prestige events and the supply of amphetamine. The task of providing security at discos in market towns with punks clustered round the war memorial fell to younger edgy men with self-conscious pony-tails and heavy work boots with designer tags. Gary in particular was openly dismissive of 'the fucking youth', and like most men approaching middle age had begun to lay down some roots in a bid to establish some security for his young family.

Viv is very large—a brave person might call him fat. However, he was a very good schoolboy boxer who still trains regularly at a local gym. He is now relatively affluent, with sufficient monetary and cultural capital to buy and sell in a plethora of local markets. He lives quietly in a council maisonette that is totally unremarkable apart from some very expensive stereo equipment and photographs of himself in the company of a famous heavyweight boxer. He has spoken on several occasions of moving out to a more salubrious area, but his roots are local and despite pressure from his girlfriend (Viv is not politically correct and when he talks of his partner he is referring to Gary, Taff, or Eric), it is difficult to imagine him living anywhere else. He has lived on the same estate for most of his life and is well known to all his neighbours, most of whom are elderly, although it is doubtful that they will have any idea of his choice of occupation.

I had been aware of Viv's existence for at least fifteen years, but we only became acquainted during the course of this research. Viv's brother had briefly been a student of mine, and when I began the research for this book I contacted him and requested that he set up an introduction. Viv had served time for a serious assault and had read some sociology while in prison. He was intrigued by the notion of somebody earning a living from the discipline, and this enabled me to negotiate access to what was obviously a crucial entrepreneurial arena. Over an Indian meal Viv explained how he would account for my presence, that I would be introduced as a friend who was out for a drink. We agreed that nobody else would be aware of my true role, that I would not take notes while in the field, nor use a tape-recorder. We then arranged to meet at midday in the Castle the following Friday.

THE CASTLE

The Castle is a Victorian pub situated in a high street where people used to shop. However, since the megastore was built, on a remote site to which buses have failed to penetrate, only the carless, immobilized by poverty or old age, spend their money here. Of the twenty-eight commercial premises adjacent to the Castle, twelve have changed hands in the last eighteen months, and seven are boarded up.

The poverty that pervades this neighbourhood lacks the theme park intensity ascribed to late twentieth-century British working-class communities by the colour supplements and television documentary makers as they relentlessly seek out an underclass to fear and pity. There are no beggars or crack addicts staining these streets, and both the young women pushing prams and their children are dressed in high-street–market-stall chic. There are few signs of inbred pathological fecundity; just poor people doing their best to get by in a landscape of mundane desolation. The media will not waste their time waiting for a riot in this high street, for it is, as photogenic as a rusting iron bar.

The Castle occupies a corner plot of this graveyard of small enterprise, and it has been hanging on for longer than its neighbours. Successive landlords have tried everything. Stag nights and hen nights, karaoke, race nights, satellite TV, lunches. Nothing has worked: you can smell it as you enter the cavernous saloon bar.

By 11.30 a.m. there are already four elderly men hunched over the racing-papers, sipping beer. They sit at separate tables, smoking roll-ups and occasionally peering over ageing spectacles.

Not that there is much to look at. Decrepit prints of fox-hunting compete with a couple of photographs of local boxers in action. But the boxers vacated the ring before keg lager became popular, and anything connected to the wall for more than a month develops on its surface a yellow film of nicotine that lends the entire pub a timeless tomblike quality. This is not a glamorous location for professional criminals to do their business, and is a long way from the glossy images that pervade fictional presentations of serious crime. By mid-day the only dubious commodities on offer in the Castle are the pies. More old men have shuffled in and located themselves unspeaking at separate tables, and it was looking increasingly as if Viv had gained his revenge upon sociology.

Just after 12.30 two men in their late twenties entered the bar, ordered beer, and made numerous calls on a mobile phone. Viv arrived, greeted me, spoke to the two men, and left. An older man in his forties with weight-lifter's shoulders and a darts-player's waistline came in and told the publican that he would be ordering something from the café later. Accompanied by a soft drink he proceeded to monopolize the pay-phone for over an hour. Viv returned with Gary, to whom I was introduced as someone interested in the work of bouncers, and once he was assured that I was not a journalist, I was dismissed along with the *Sporting Life* scholars as part of the backdrop to their skulduggery.

Then Eric arrived, extremely suspicious about my presence. Viv dismissed me as a teacher, and Eric went to work on his phone. All of the firm are dressed in American casual clothes that imply rather more about the wearer than competent shopping technique. With the exception of one of the teenage gofers who has a pony-tail, the Firm wear their hair unremarkably short. Eric has parallel lines razored on to his scalp which complement the long scar on his chin.

A group of office-workers in ill-fitting suits steel themselves for the afternoon by drinking pints of cider, and the man with weight-lifter's shoulders orders the all-day breakfast from the café next door, consuming the meal standing up at the pay-phone. Viv later told me that the man works in the ex-seamen's hostel and 'likes a bet'. Three men in their teens arrived and sat quietly in a corner, until Eric handed over some keys to the smallest of them, who left the pub, returning a few minutes later.

At about 2.15 a tall man in his forties arrived with a woman, both sporting heavy suntans. Gary bought them drinks and they retired to a far corner of the pub where the woman dominated the conversation. Gary, Eric, and one of the younger men left with the woman, and the man stayed behind to order a gin and tonic. When Gary, Eric, and their gofer returned a few minutes later, the tanned man swigged his drink, shook hands with the two younger men, and left. The two ex-football hooligans were ecstatic; they had obviously done a deal, but at this stage it was difficult to see regarding what.

For the rest of the afternoon the members of the firm huddled in corners or paced the room mumbling into mobile phones, while the old men were freeze-framed over their Guinness and fantasy accumulators. The three younger men were regularly sent on errands, which took them but a few minutes, and the café next door kept sending in meals. Very little alcohol was consumed, and since the departure of the tanned couple, the veins on Eric's neck looked close to bursting. By six o'clock the day's dealing was over, the office-workers were back on cider, and three women from the freezer centre across the road came in to drink lager in their break from the prawns and black forest gateau. Viv left just after five, and the rest of the firm melted away when the evening trade started to arrive.

At this stage I did not understand what was going on. I knew that drugs were involved, but how the firm were operating was not clear. Viv had agreed to meet me the next day, but failed to turn up. His mobile phone was turned off, and I had no way of contacting him. The following Friday I sat in the café opposite the Castle in an attempt to bulk up before the lagers, and from a seat by the window Gary and Eric's operation made perfect sense. Orders were being taken over the phone and delivered or picked up from the boots of three ancient cars parked close by. The cars never moved; they were merely storage. When I entered the Castle somewhat enlightened and with a significantly increased cholesterol count, Viv was surprised to see me and made no attempt to account for his non-appearance the previous week. The clientele was identical, with the exception of Eric, whose absence seemed ominous. Viv was obviously tense as a result of my presence, and after a very long hour, during which I was able to observe the various roles of the firms members, I left.

A month later and the Friday lunch-time trade is apparently back to normal. The old boys are working on their accumulators, and the suits in the corner are in their cider stage. There are no drug demons or mobile phones, and a television is on in the top corner of the room relaying an Australian soap to nobody in particular. The firm's non-appearance is worrying: if they have been arrested the light of suspicion could easily shine on me. Although I cannot be certain, I think the old cars used for storage have gone. The woman working behind the bar tells me that I am not the first to enquire after Gary.

Nearly six months later I bumped into Viv at a football match. By then he was a season-ticket holder, the kind to demand the public flogging of hooligans. He was looking affluent and was keen to talk. When we met at his home two days later, his rendition of the firm's fortunes contained a few unexpected twists. The firm had disintegrated when Gary was arrested, and Gary had carefully guarded the source of his amphetamines. Eric had tried to keep the firm viable by working up his own contacts, but he was starting from scratch and proved unsuccessful. Viv and Taff had left the security business and set up in silk-screening, producing high-quality copies of designer T-shirts. Gary was serving a sentence for an assault on a waiter after a fight in a late night restaurant. He claimed that the fight was instigated by a group of off-duty policemen as part of a long-standing feud between his family and the local police station. Viv pointed out that if Eric had been present they both would be serving life sentences by now.

The list of legitimate businesses fed by capital and connections established as a result of football hooliganism is extensive, and every group of early to mid-1980s terrace veterans has its own stories of blood and money. Ex-hooligans of Gary and Eric's generation have made their mark on show business, the building industry, the property industry at home and abroad, catering, and a whole range of disparate enterprises. Some of these men have become seriously rich, some are in prison, and others continue to grind out the villainy in more mundane arenas.

The firm was no more, although Eric was still free to explore the limits of his talents. Almost two years later one Saturday afternoon I was taking my son to a football match at the ground where, Eric, Gary, Viv, and Taff had forged their reputations ten years before. Eric was next to a transit van outside a Pakistani-owned off-licence. He doesn't seem to be interested in football any more, the beautiful game having lost out to more worldly pursuits. One of the gofers from the Castle apologetically explains something to him, and Eric fixes on the metal grille on the shop's door: 'Does he want the fucking lager or what?'

7

Buck the Market: Crime, Pleasure, and Gentlemen of Leisure

> He that makes his pleasure be his business will never make his business be
> a pleasure.
>
> > (Daniel Defoe)

But some people can at least try. It is important that we are not carried away
with the seductive, and at times hackneyed, tendency to view all serious crime
as a highly rational activity, driven purely by commercial imperatives. We should
consider carefully the pursuit of pleasure that not only provides the spur to
engage in a criminal career, but also drives many individuals to gain sufficient
levels of competence and consistency to maintain a life-style which for non-
criminals can only be aspired to at designated times, within regulated spaces,
and with highly restrained moral and material resources.

These essentially hedonistic choices of life-style, these compulsions and commitments, set apart professional crime from the mundane rhythms of legitimate
employment. This chapter is concerned with the relationship between professional crime and some of those choices, compulsions, and commitments.

PARTY TIME: JASON'S STORY

Jason likes to have a good time. Day and night, week in and week out, the
pursuit of pleasure dominates his waking hours. He defines himself not in terms
of criminality, but in terms of a single-minded hedonism that is enabled by
crime. Crime not only finances his leisure however, it also swamps it, filling up
his party-time with a perpetual hustle. Money is needed to invest in leisure,
rather than to acquire power, or establish resilience in the market-place. Crime
for Jason is a means to an end, a rational engagement with the market that is
purely instrumental in that it conveys with it the promise of a seven-day weekend.

Jason chose to be a drug-dealer, a role that had brought with it both success
and failure.

We was doing so well. We was making bundles of money and you couldn't see an end
to it. I could go anywhere and party with the money we had, and everybody they knew
us. . . . They loved us, wanted us everywhere. None of it was a problem to us. We could
just go from party to party to club and that. The women was there all the time. I tell you,

we had such a good time, you see we were the ones with everything, and they loved us for it.

The main reason was we never dealt with nobody who we knew couldn't come up with the dough. All the time they come to us for a deal of this or that and it was 'Right, well that's a monkey so I'll see you the day after tomorrow.' We never stood for it. It was money up front or fuck off, and there was so many people trying to get in on it that we never went without customers. There was people lining up some nights to hand over money for stuff they never . . . You understand what I'm saying? It was enough to just be seen buying the gear from us, you understand me. What it did for them never meant too much I don't think. A lot of the white people like to come to us and be seen, well, just, I don't know, being with us. Parties, and we go and enjoy ourselves, but also we took the money—that's why we was there.

During the early eighties Jason had been a successful drug-dealer working initially in the Midlands before moving to London to set up home with a woman he had met on holiday in Ibiza. Jason's parents were originally from different islands in the Caribbean and both arrived in London in the late 1950s. They met and married while working for London Transport, and Jason was the first of three children. When he was 9 or 10 the family moved to the Midlands, where they stayed until Jason's mother and sister returned to the Caribbean.

Jason left school a year later with five high-grade GCSEs, and a rare and highly prized engineering apprenticeship.

I was dealing dope like most of us. We was smoking and, if you can call it dealing, there was hardly any mark-up just for your spars at the weekend.

The apprenticeship faltered, apparently through boredom, and the cannabis-dealing became increasingly important, although Jason denies that at this stage his involvement was anything more than peripheral.

All I was doing was teaming up with a spar and buying an ounce, or if we was flush, more, but not a lot . . . We marked it up according to who they was. Sometimes we would get a bit saucy and go to the student pubs. Tell you, sell anything to them; they was round us saying 'What you got?' Dope, they bought poppers, poppers! They tell us what they want and we jump in a cab and buy from a shop, ten minutes and we are back . . . So stupid I tell you, they making like it's Charlie [cocaine]. We just fall out of there and go clubbing.

In response to my questions about money Jason insisted that the tape-recorder be turned off. His reticence emerged as a desire to keep his success in perspective. He insisted that at this time he was making very little money from dealing in drugs: others were making more, driving bigger cars, and wearing more jewellery. Yet his denial of material success has little to do with false modesty. The period that I spent talking to him coincided with media speculation about drug-dealing and violence amongst the black community, and in particular the role of yardies. As a black male who had been active in the drug trade for a decade, Jason was keen to distance himself from the black-gangster stereotype.

However, some measure of his success can be gleaned from the fact that in the mid-1980s, at the age 20, he owned a second-hand BMW and financed a visit to his mother for himself and his father and brother. However, the bulk of Jason's money was spent on 'dope, clothes, and nice wheels'.

By this time Jason was formally employed as a minicab driver, an occupation that gave him a certain licence to be driving the streets of his Midland town at all times of the day and night.

The controller, he was the guvnor, and he knew what I was about. For a while I paid him when I never worked . . . If he gave me a job when I was at my business, I would turn it down and drop the man a tenner to keep me on the firm.

Later Jason found that his boss could only maintain the long hours spent in the control room by constantly dabbing his fingers into a bag of amphetamine powder. Jason started to supply him, and in turn the minicab boss became a useful cipher for new customers. Jason also used speed to enhance both work and recreation. The pace of his life increased and so did the profits.

It weren't a black thing. I do apologise for going on, but you must understand that speed it was such a common thing for everyone. Well, it still is, because it gives you the legs to do whatever it is you are doing. So when the speed thing got going I was selling to everybody. Anybody who wanted. . . . I was buying from whites, and they was always the people who was earning in a way that could really make a difference to the way they live.

By 'making a difference', Jason was referring to the ostentatious life-styles that could be bought by dealers who operated some distance away from the street. One dealer in particular caught Jason's imagination.

A white man with a Liverpool thing [accent]. I only ever had enough for a couple of deals with him, but he would meet at the service station. Man pulls up at the service station in this monster Merc. He gets out and he is about the age what I am now . . . got a black suit on and a black woolly hat. Everybody said that he had a pit bull in the back seat. So one day he puts the bag in my boot, and then I just have a look and it's a cat, a cat in the back just lying there looking up. But you could only do a deal with him if you was like really holding, you understand me? And then it was hard, he was always engaged. He did big business all over, and you had to be lucky to catch him, but if you did and you had to have the money, then the whiz you got the best I ever had without doubt.

And his customers?

At that time there was a lot of Paki shop people who work all day and all night. These were fairly young like; they had straight businesses. I did a lot of trade with those people . . . I was making money, more than a lot. Yes, but I was no big time, and I was really pushing myself. I was taking calls and making deliveries so it got fucking stupid. . . . No time to have a time for myself. I was always working. And then there got so many people at it that I was always looking for more to buy, and picking it up and all that. And not just the Paki people. There was a lot of people just wanted to get into it, and it was sweet way of making money.

Like several other respondents in this book, the convergence of late eighties youth and enterprise cultures opened up an Aladdin's cave of money-making possibilities. Jason had been unhappy at home for some time, and he was constantly clashing with his father. Consequently, when a group of friends decided to spend the summer in Ibiza, he did not hesitate to join them. Initially the trip was regarded as a holiday, a short break from the hectic pace of work and play that had driven Jason. He stayed for a year, living initially on savings, and then on selling counterfeit drugs to gullible tourists. He came home with a new partner and an intricate knowledge of what became known as rave culture and the ideological contours of the substances that sustained it. Jason set up home in south London with his new partner, a white social-work student with a university education who came from the West Country. Jason sold ecstasy and speed at raves all over London and the south-east.

Best time for me without a doubt. I was working with all the top people. A lot had been in Ibiza and we knew each other, so when it came to setting up here it was easy, all anybody wanted was to have a good time. It was a time when there was no worries, and that was the E. Not only that, but people wanted to have a party, and it was a good time for me—not just the money, but the people . . . And I was one of the, well, not one of the main people, because there was so many at this time who was making money, but I was doing people for ecstasy for about, I suppose, less than a year.

Then there was that shooting at the place in Surrey. Then it started to change. You could feel it was different. The people I was with, they just faded out of it, and I was turning up, and the new people . . . it was guns, baseball bats. Security, but if you weren't working with them they just rob you, I tell you. Understand me—a couple of times they tax me of everything I have right in the car park. There was some bad lickings at these places. I lost a lot of money and things started to go to the fucking wall for me, you understand.

In 1991 Jason was convicted of wounding a man in a south London club. He had retained his suppliers from the 'summer of love', but, forced to explore more traditional outlets for his goods, had encountered marketing difficulties that were matched by his problems at home. His partner's return to the West Country coincided with the death of Jason's father, and the role of freelance dealer was proving wearing for a young man who was beginning to sense the limits to which a lone trader in the drugs business might aspire.

It was when I went back home [to the Midlands] that it made sense to me. There at first they treat me like the big nob from London, and everybody was round me for gear. But after a while, you understand, the deals they could get local was better and that was that. I was just scrambling about with all the others. Good week, bad week, and soon I come back to the flat. Kid brother moved down and he gets this job. So I am back with the same people. . . . Now, understand me right, I should have been more careful when I had money, but I did the gold thing and the nice motor instead. So when something big come up I could never put it down. I was doing the clubs and having a good time, especially with the Charlie. Now I don't mean to disrespect you, but you wouldn't know with

Charlie just what a life it give you. But I never think only in what sort of night it give me. And then it was 'Give me this, and I sell that', and then I got enough to enjoy myself, you understand me, have a good time.

Although he aspired to cocaine-dealing, he remained a dealer in amphetamines and ecstasy, selling in pubs and clubs while leading a hectic social life. Then Jason stabbed a man when he was confronted over non-payment of a debt. When questioned about the stabbing he was certainly more matter of fact on the subject of violence than any other respondent in this book.

I owe the man something around £500. Now these are not gangster-men, no heavy people, and I reckon, well, no problem, I was doing all right. But it was Charlie really that the people was wanting. I was not getting to do anything with the E. I had to be real. You could get it anywhere, you understand. By the time I was getting there, people undercut me by plenty. Sometimes I was buying for one and selling for one. That did happen. I could never get the money together for enough to make it cheap, and I just go fuck. So I get 5 here, 10 there, and pay one back with the other. I just keep moving and hope that it all don't just meet up together.

But it did, and Jason stabbed the debt-collector in the shoulder. According to some acquaintances of Jason, he had been extremely successful at exploiting 'the black thing', and passing off ordinary cannabis as the highly sought after, and expensive, semsillia. This was the cause of the dispute that led to the stabbing incident. When I returned to Jason to ask him about this, he again asked me to turn the tape-recorder off. He explained that the ruse was very common, and that he had indeed worked it upon the man he had stabbed, a man to whom he also owed £500. But as Jason explained,

He was game for a laugh. It's just the way it goes. I don't make the rules. It happen to me all the time. All I ever wanted was a good time.

Less than a year after his release, Jason now lives in a bedsit in his cousin's home, and is back on the minicabs, driving his cousin's car at night.

And when you drive about at night you see the money people make. . . . You understand me, all I'm thinking is 'I want that so I can have a good time.' Is no good to me when I am a old man. Even now I go for a party and move a little shit here, 'cos people always ask for it, understand? Ain't going to be cabbing for long. If people want to trade with you, you can't stop them. If I want to make some money to have a time, some wheels, and a party then—I won't stay the cabs for too long. I got some stuff going on get me back. The way I want to live cost me money. A good time cost money.

THIRSTY WORK: TEDDY'S STORY

Teddy was an enthusiastic subject to research.

You fucking come and see me, fucking write about me, you fucking long streak of fucking useless—Come and put this in a fucking book, fucking Professor fucking Thunderbirds Brains.

He was also exceptionally easy to find, as he always left in his wake a powerful and all-pervasive reek of cheap aftershave, traces of which hung over any pub that he had visited in the previous forty-eight hours. Worse, it clung to your clothes entered every pore of your skin, and lurked dangerously in an alcove at the back of your throat that would effectively suspend the desire to consume solids.

Teddy is of indeterminate age, presenting a collage of skin-types and styles that span a number of decades. The outstanding feature of his appearance is his hair. This is big hair à la mod, a carefully coiffured busby of blond highlights that has its origins in early sixties sexual ambiguity, ciphered through working-class hippie and glam-rock styles, and running to ground in the late seventies with a professional footballer's demi-perm. It is always immaculate, albeit a little over long at the back, the sideburns densely Edwardian rather than fash-ionably angular and spivish. This frames a face that resembles a map of the British Empire *circa* 1920. Irregular red blotches decorate a visage of uncom-promising peaks and valleys dominated by a pitted and carelessly arranged nose. Teddy always wears a suit, tight of beam and wide of lapel. A dark polo-necked shirt serves to emphasize the bulbous neck, and the whole is topped off by a sheepskin coat whose stains defy forensic analysis.

Teddy is known as someone who would steal anything. In the early eighties he stole a bus from a local depot when late one night he experienced some trouble hailing a cab. Similarly, he had once entered an off licence with the intention of buying some lager, only to emerge some minutes later with a case of vodka on his shoulder, pilfered while the shop's owner toiled in the stock-room. But this was just for fun, the kind of opportunistic self-gratification that merely papers over the cracks in Teddy's seamless web of serious criminality.

As a youth he had worked on the 'find the lady' card scam in London's West End. He worked with friends and family as a look-out and general jostler, while punters were relieved of their money under the misapprehension that they were gambling. As a consequence, Teddy met pickpockets, prostitutes, and gangsters, and became acquainted with a variety of money-making opportunities. He sold fake gold and jewellery, often mixed with the proceeds of burglaries, to jewel-lers and naïve fences. He worked on long frauds, and plundered lorries, ware-houses, and offices. The reputation of Teddy's family, a sprawling brood of fighters and drinkers whose notoriety spanned four generations, was insurance against complaints from dissatisfied customers. Their lineage includes a grand-mother who smoked a pipe and fought men in the street when emerging from the pub on Sunday afternoons. They made their own entertainment in those days.

Teddy took to burglary and borstal, before a cousin set up an illegal drinking-club in the basement of a Turkish-owned clothing factory. The club provided a base for his family and their cohorts, and Teddy applied himself to stocking the bar. There were a number of strategies involved. Theft was the most obvious, and the family were always on the look-out for stolen whisky in particular.

Teddy's major success was in his collaboration with a schoolfriend whose father had worked all his life in a gin distillery. One of the long-standing scams involved the theft of labels, which were then stuck on bottles containing a potent home-brew that when diluted with a mixer tasted approximately like gin. This was usually a once-a-year collaboration with a handful of local pubs, designed to exploit the indiscriminate Christmas imbiber. Teddy and his cohorts took this a step further, printing thousands of labels and obtaining facsimile bottles and cartons, before setting up a business selling 'stolen' gin to pubs and clubs all over London. Unfortunately Teddy sold his moonshine without explaining its true origins to a notorious firm who owned a number of local spielers. This was regarded as a gross insult and the beating that Teddy received has, with the passing of the years, assumed epic intensity, and the stoic manner with which he accepted his punishment established him as a 'face' in all the right places for all the wrong reasons. After he recovered Teddy collaborated with his assailants on a number of scams including the supply of moonshine gin.

However, his main money-making venture by the mid-1960s was a variation on the corner game. This involved selling goods that did not exist to buyers who, after handing over their money, would find cigarette cartons full of old news-paper, or that the washing-machines or televisions were never delivered. As the buyer believed that the goods were stolen, the police were irrelevant. He was minding the door of a club in Soho, working the corner game and selling fake diamond rings, when he was convicted for receiving stolen goods.

There is a gap of about seven years for which it became impossible to glean any information concerning his whereabouts. From the late 1960s to the mid-1970s Teddy was apparently invisible. However, during this time his family had began to disintegrate as a result of a number of long prison sentences, rehousing, and the violent death of one of its stalwarts.

From the mid-1970s to the present Teddy has owned shops selling second-hand goods, and been active in the supply of forged MOT certificates. Every afternoon he alternates between the betting-shop and the pub next door, the coherence of the various deals that he completes along the way declining as his alcohol intake increases. His main weakness is buying stolen car radios with a view to selling them in one of his shops. The pubescent thieves wait until Teddy has made it through to the alcohol-inspired virtual reality of the last race before clinching the price of a night's sulphate.

Teddy has been an active committed criminal for over thirty years. Along the way he has served a number of prison sentences but he has no speciality, no discernible skill. He is a 'rounder' of the old school who lives to drink and gamble. To most of the locals he is a bit of a joke, but nobody is likely to be laughing to his face. He still has enough clout to be treated with a modicum of respect, and his ability to remain in business through four decades of unremitting skulduggery tempers the fact that he has never come close to retiring to a villa on the Costa del Sol.

Today Teddy rents a flat above a supermarket from his nephew. It is within stumbling distance of the pub and the betting-shop. He is still making a living and central to his personal style there remains an unpredictable edge that makes him dangerous to ignore. One day that accumulator at Sandown, York, or Kempton Park will come off, and until then the MOT certificates are good earners.

EACH WAY BETS, AND REFLECTIONS ON PENAL
POLICY: JOCK'S STORY

Accumulators

Gambling was very important. It took up such a large part of my life. Because you played snooker for money, when you weren't playing snooker for money you were reading form for the horses, which I took very seriously because it's not about sticking pins in newspapers, it's—ask any horse player—it's a serious business. You're putting your own judgement on the line. Then you were picking out the horses you were going to bet, then you'd be in the betting-shop in the afternoon. So from getting up, certainly until late afternoon, everything revolved around gambling. . . .

Obviously if you've got no money, you can't gamble. The two then start interacting. You commit crime to get the money to gamble. If you gamble, you lose the money, so you commit crime to get the money back, and so on and so on. Obviously on occasions the reverse would be true. You'd have a win, you wouldn't need to go and commit crime.

By his own admission Jock did not take naturally to the world of work. Leaving school and entering the halcyon labour market of the mid-1960s, he quickly developed leisure tastes that were at odds with white-collar respectability. A grammar school boy from an unremarkable working-class background, Jock was heading for fifty years of clerical porridge when he discovered the joy of 'kiting'.

When I was at it in mid- to late sixties, you had all that swinging sixties atmosphere, this idea that anything was possible, all very hedonistic, lots of money about and the whole sort of culture that was very anti-work. For people who wanted to work it was easy— you could get two jobs in the same day. You could go down the Labour Exchange in the morning, get a job; if you didn't like it, you could go and get another one in the afternoon.

I didn't want to go to university because I thought that was just another three years of school. I in fact joined the Civil Service, and because I only had 'O' levels I could only go in at a certain grade, and although I got to do good work and I know that I was well thought of, I could also see that without a degree, all my career horizons were strictly limited. . . . Basically, I got frustrated with the whole idea of work, and not being able to get the promotion that I thought I should get, all that sort of thing, and I got disillusioned with it and left the Civil Service, thought I'd try the private sector. . . . The only difference was that it was more repetitive and boring.

With his long-term job prospects so unappealing, Jock was forced to reflect on what he really wanted from life.

Basically, I felt that I wanted money. That's what you were brought up to believe. Money was important to you and really I suppose I never found a way of getting hold of any of it legitimately that appealed. Either if I had something I liked doing there wasn't enough money, or if there was something that was well paid it was awful work, and in the end you just get to thinking there must be an easier way.

I'd had my first little taste of LSD and smoking pot and all that sort of thing, and it seemed to me on the one hand you could get up at a stupid hour in the morning, go and cram yourself into a train, and go and do a job that you didn't like, mixing with people that you wouldn't choose to; or you could go over the park and take drugs and play snooker and gamble, which seemed to be far more a better way of spending your time to me. But it needed money.

Having reached such a stark conclusion, Jock set about seeking an alternative path that would lead him to his nirvana.

Things started in the snooker hall really. Most of the lads in there, they had their little games; they were ducking and diving one way or another, so we're talking mainly scallywags there, birds of a feather, that sort of thing. You do tend to mix with your own. . . . People have their games and it is, it's its own little culture.

I used to do cheque books, I started off with cheque books. Like a lot of lads, we used to get into the snooker hall, the local snooker hall. In those days that was the sign of the classic misspent youth not like it is now, and that's where I started. I knew a couple of people who were doing cheques, and it seemed like easy work—I give it a try and it was.

Now where I was at —— [work], I got matey with somebody there who used to work in a bank and he had one of these £30 cheque guarantee cards which had just been started at the banks. We both had a bit of a hard time at the Cheltenham races, so we were both short of money and I said 'Well, what say you give me your cheque book and card and I'll go and see what I can do with it,' and that's how it all started. . . . I practised his signature for a few days and we arranged to do it on the very last day that I worked there. I'd already given in my notice, and I thought, well, what better alibi could I have other than to say I was at work, and I knew nobody would be keeping an eye on me because it was a big place. I was going round tidying up last bits and pieces with different people, saying goodbye, all this sort of thing, and then there was going to be a drink in the pub in the afternoon. So I set out about ten o'clock, disappeared for something like three hours with this guy's cheque book and card, headed off to Westminster, which I knew really well because I'd worked there, hit as many banks there as I could. Went in to the West End, did a few more there, came back in time for my own farewell drinks party at work, and everybody as far as they were concerned I'd been in the building the whole morning. So there I was with a pocketful of the bank's money which was the equivalent of about six months' pay net. I think it was £270, I think I did nine banks. Because this was the Midland Bank, you couldn't go into any bank. You had to go to the one who'd issued the card. And I think it was £270, which, as I say, was something like about six months' net salary I got in those about three hours. The adrenaline was just pouring through me and I can remember at the same time Dave, who I was in cahoots with, standing there giving 'Where's my wallet? Oh no, I've lost my wallet and cheque book.' . . . He then had to phone the bank and phone the police. He also told the security guard in —— and the security guard apparently had said to him 'Oh well, if you've lost it here I shouldn't have any worries about it, because nobody here would have the nerve to go and do anything with it.' That to me was almost as good as the money itself. I felt as though here I was, I'd fucked the system, I'd got six months' money in three hours out of this place. They all thought that people who worked there wouldn't be capable of doing something like that. It just added to the whole buzz of the thing.

As for legitimate work, that option was now behind him. Jock retired early. If work was merely a means of acquiring money it made little sense, in the face of these new opportunities, to keep up the nine-to-five routine. He was now only interested in those activities 'that financed me being able to take drugs, play snooker, and gamble instead of going to work'.

Shopping

Jock's targets reflected his desire to achieve a quick turn-round and rapid cash return. Once the goods had been acquired there seemed little point in magnifying the risk of being apprehended by attempting to fence valuable and therefore traceable goods. The risk of capture was restricted to the point of purchase, or, in the case of withdrawing money from banks, engaging and disengaging from a transaction. These were also the points at which Jock's growing competencies were yielding rewards of a less obvious nature.

We used to do off licences, supermarkets for drink, record shops, that sort of thing—anything where we could get an instant sale at two-thirds to half-price, knock them out the same day. The first thing that I did, I was very nervous, but then I got the money, nobody batted an eyelid, and it just got easier and easier and easier each time. First of all you'd be nervous. They'd be standing there watching you sign the thing and you'd be a little bit shaky perhaps. But then after the first two or three have gone all right, I have to say it was thoroughly enjoyable. Going into a bank they'd say 'How would you like your money sir?' and you'd say 'Quickly as possible please.' (Laughs.) They'd hand it over and it was so easy it was enjoyable and it was half the buzz. At the end of the day you come back and you got pocketfuls of the bank's money and this great feeling. That was half of it, half the fun—the feeling you got out of it. It wasn't just the money. It was the feeling that you'd got hold of all this money so easy—hadn't hurt anyone. It was like you'd beat the system.

The Moody Lose

The arrangements that enabled Jock to be in possession of someone else's cheque book and card were equally simple. The spoils were modest but consistent, and when distributed reflected an acknowledgement of emotional strain as well as criminal commitment.

What I used to do, it would be if you arrange with someone to lose their book—'moody lose' their book and card to you—so then you knew you had all day because it would be pre-arranged that they wouldn't phone up the bank until sort of quarter past three or something. You knew you had a full day in front of you. . . . I used to work it fifty-fifty because if anything I was getting the easier end of the deal, 'cos it was so easy getting the money from the banks, and it seemed to me that the nasty part of the deal was when he would be faced by the police and given a grilling. . . . So as far as I was concerned they were earning half the money as I was.

You could also get just an ordinary cheque book and you could go round banks because the loss of a cheque book wouldn't be circulated in those days—they would think it was of no consequence. And you could go round different branches of a bank, stick a cheque over for, say, £20, and say 'I've got an agreement,' because in those days because they didn't have so many of these cards, people would have an account near where they lived and they'd have an agreement with a branch where they worked so they could draw a certain amount of money each week or each month, and I used to find that probably six out of ten they'd just hand it, no question at all.

They'd pay you the money. The other four they would go and look in some little file to see if there was a card there and say 'We can't find the reference.' Then you'd have to pull up and say, 'Isn't this the so-and-so branch? Oh, I've made a mistake,' or whatever. So that was that.

Bankers

Jock acknowledges that the technology of the early 1960s was easily exploited by anyone sufficiently committed.

And you'd also find in those days—hard to believe now—that you could get things in shops. 'Do you take a cheque?' Quite a few would say 'Yes, OK, put your name and address on the back.' It sounds totally naïve by today's standards, but you could do that sort of thing. You get one of those cheque card guarantee things. They'd only just started up—we're talking sort of over twenty years ago—and there wasn't any of the business of fiddling about with the flyleaves at the back they have now with stamps, or poking biros through it, and all that game. You could just go round with a clean cheque book and a card and if you were quick you could do all thirty in a day.

Obviously after a few years of this things all started getting a lot tighter. Banks started introducing the flysheet in the back of the cheque book so that they could poke biros through the day, or they could stamp the thing, that sort of thing. Also I have to say it used to get a bit tiresome, what was enjoyable first of all, first few times I did it, hammering round twenty, twenty-five, thirty banks. . . . You've got to work, and the enjoyment started going out of it, although the rewards were still good.

The Double Shuffle

Jock's response to improved technology and security was classically simple.

But what I found was a really good method in the end was that you had to open a false account, which was quite difficult because you had to give references and you had to have access to an address somewhere, but it was possible. Once you'd got a false account opened up and running and you'd got a cheque book, then you got hold of as much money as you could. Sometimes I'd have to borrow it—£500 or something like that. Stick it all into the account, then you go in with a cheque for, say, £500 or whatever it was that you had in there; hand it over. They would say 'Just a minute, sir.' Off they'd go and look into this great big daily print-out of all the accounts, look down balance—£502, whatever—they'd come back, 'How would you like the money?', and pay it out.

You'd give it an hour, wait until that person was no longer on the ramp, then you'd go in again. Now you write down the account number on a piece of paper, and you write out another cheque for the £500 or whatever, you go up to the cashier, give them the account number, and say to them 'Could you tell me what the balance is on that account, please.' So then they go and check. The worst way they come back and say it's £2.02 and you go 'Oh, I thought it was more than that. Thank you.' But actually it never happened, because it would always be they'd come back and there would be £502. So there's the next cheque £500. So the beauty of it was that you were getting the money in one hit, and also you couldn't really get caught, because by asking them on the second visit 'What's the balance?' you would know whether or not the balance had been altered. But, as I say, it actually never had.

Life-style

Jock had achieved his desired life-style, and articulately acknowledges the essential ambiguity of its various elements.

Used to have a nice lay-in till about eleven or twelve. Most days head off to the billiard hall, see the lads, and have a few games of snooker or whatever was going on there, cards. Betting-shop in the afternoon, then in the evenings it would probably be out to see some music somewhere, drugs, what have you. It was actually quite a bit schizophrenic, because all the scallywags in the billiard hall, a lot of them were a bit older than me . . . ducking and diving and all that sort of thing. . . . Weren't into the drugs or anything like that, non-judgemental about it, but just don't want to know.

The other half was mixing with the flower people, hippies. They'd be over the park being beautiful people, and they couldn't understand all of this stuff about snooker and betting-shops and billiard halls. It was like having one foot in two totally different, almost mutually exclusive worlds, but both of them in their way deviant, both of them unconventional. And that really was the key. It was all about revenge, I suppose, not wanting to conform to that 'Put on a suit, get your hair cut, and go and be a wage slave.' Anything to get away from that.

Nicked

Although prison was something of an inevitability the reality of incarceration came as something of a shock. Indeed his experiences as a convict have inspired something akin to a 'left realist' response to penality that Jock is now exploring via the world of academe.

Basically, getting nicked. That went wrong. I've been nicked a couple of times on the way, because by now I've been doing this for four or five years. The first couple of times I got nicked, you know you go through the sort of ladder of sentences. The first time you get fined, then the next time I got a suspended sentence, and each time I went to court there was something unreal about it. Every time you walked away, it was as though nothing really has happened. All right, you got a fine, so you've got to find a few quid to pay it—go and do another job. Suspended sentence. 'Oh, I'll have to be a bit more careful.' I suppose it was that got me into this idea of doing this double shuffle, this double withdrawal thing. . . . But I mean, I told too many people my business really, too many people got to find out my business. So after I'd done a few of these double shuffles . . . a couple of mates who were seriously in with me, we wanted to go away, do some travelling, which is what we did. . . .

That was easier than you could believe. All the money we had we pooled together so one of us got a whole book of American Express travellers' cheques. Got as far as Rome, declared them lost, got them replaced, cashed all the replacements. Then we went to Athens, somebody else with the cash would then buy another set, pop off to one of the islands, and come back with another set and declare them lost and then get another set.

I remember we finally actually ran out of money in Afghanistan and ended up trading in all these knocked-off cheques to a money-lender, money-changer, and then scooting off to India. But I felt very uncomfortable because we wouldn't be dealing with PC 49 here. There'd be some geezer with a scimitar to cut your throat if he'd got his hands on you. We needed some more money anyway. One of them had jumped bail, one of them was wanted by the police, money-lenders, by all sorts of people back in England, so I said, well, all right I'll go back, 'cos it's easier, as I was clear.

As soon as I got to Heathrow the police were there. 'Someone in the police in Chadwell Heath wants to see you, has been wanting to see you since October or something.' The last job I'd done was November, just before we'd set off, and the funny thing was that the copper at Heathrow couldn't find out anything, and had no reason to detain me. So I went, but I got the name of this geezer in Chadwell Heath who was trying to see me, or wanted to see me, and I've been phoning him up, and every time I phoned him up and said 'I want to speak to DC ——,' they go 'Oh no, he's out on a special job, he won't be back for weeks, maybe months.' And it turned out the special job he was on was me. (Laughs.) 'Cos while I was away one of the people who knew my business who was on the fringe of what was going on had been nicked for something . . . they started coming all the heavy with him about 'We've got this down to you, this down to you,' all this sort of stuff. So he'd started talking and my name had come up, so that was it. Eventually I got nicked . . . and because I was still in breach of a suspended by then and this was now a conspiracy, all the rest of it, so that was my first taste of Her Majesty's hospitality. At that point I thought, well . . .

I got eighteen months, and it's an unfashionable viewpoint, but I have to say that on the one hand I felt that was right. I had no quibble about the fact that I'd got a prison sentence, or the length. I figured that I was about right, this was justice. In the first few weeks in Wormwood Scrubs, which is not the pleasantest place, there's a lot of time in the cell to reflect. . . . The very birth of the penitentiary and John Howard and Jeremy Bentham, the idea that the prison puts a man in touch either with his conscience or his reason, and they weren't wrong. Because when you're stuck in the prison cell lying on the bed, you start to think things like 'What the fuck did I do to get here?' And I think if you accept the fact that you're not going to kid anyone in that situation, you accept the fact, well yes, it was me, what I did, that put me here. I think far more criminals would accept that and be prepared to admit that than most people would give credit for. It was certainly true in my case, and it was, if you like, a deterrent, because I thought, if I carry on, they've got my number now, and all that would mean is the sentences would just get longer.

Criminal Records

I got nicked 'cos I done something stupid and I done something stupid 'cos I really needed the money quick. So I thought, can't have that again, better stabilize, get a job, so I can take me time more.

Jock eased into a job with a record distribution company.

Now all the kids, long hair, all the beautiful people, whatever, used to go getting bit of casual work there, picking records, packing them, that sort of thing. I thought, that will do me, I'll do that for a couple of months just to keep myself straight. So I turned up there and said 'Have you got any work going?' and they gave me an application form and I filled it out, and the next thing I know there's a feller in a suit standing there saying 'Hello. Three and a half years' Civil Service, year and a bit —— and ——, done a little bit of data-related work in computers, so the next thing I'm working in an office. . . .

So basically I was autonomous, I had my own personal little agenda, I used to carry on my own business with nobody looking over my shoulder at all. And of course, being that way inclined, and after something for nothing at any given opportunity, one of the first thoughts I had when I was there, you see all these masses and masses of records and tapes and everything, I thought, well, must be a little fiddle here. What I used to do then, because nobody else really knew quite what I was about, I used to walk around in my suit and a clipboard and a pen and I'd go walking up and down all these big banks of tapes where all the tapes were stored, and then someone else from the office would come down a flight of stairs and they'd see me doing this and say 'Oh, what you nicking the tapes again mate?' and I'd go 'Yeah', and of course as soon as they were out of sight that's exactly what I was doing, I was nicking the tapes. . . . I used to fill up all the pockets of my suit with all these tapes, and then when you come in and leave you go through the passenger lifts for the shop, and the company had a couple of security guys standing around at the bottom, and when people came out, like the pickers and the packers, every once in a while they'd frisk them, they'd search them to see if they'd got any nicked stuff. Of course I come out with my suit walking so slow in case I rattled with all these tapes that I've got in my pockets and everything, and they'd be giving it 'Goodnight, sir, have a nice weekend', and I'd be going 'Yeah, same to you. Thank you. Goodnight.'

Then the next thing, I thought, well, I got in cahoots with one of my mates, and he used to come in posing as a shopper with a big brown box under his arm, and he'd go up to one of the guards and say 'Excuse me, can you tell me what floor the telephone tables are on.' Up he'd come, meet me in one of the toilets somewhere, standing there with a box of fifty cassettes, which he would then stick in this box he brought in with him, and walk out as a customer of the store. So that was the next step in the operation.

Because some of me mates were selling bootleg records. They were into making bootleg records of Dylan and Hendrix and all this sort of stuff, and selling them to shops, so they knew a lot of record shops that were dodgy, so I had a lot of potential clients for half-price credit notes, and that's what I started doing. Sometimes I'd forge other people's signatures who were authorized to make credit notes, sometimes I'd do it myself. . . . And it worked sweet as a nut—no problem—and I must have been getting I suppose £50–£60 a week out of this, which I suppose was two or three times what my salary was.

And then the next step was that —— ——, who had —— Records, which all it was at the time was a big mail order company. Because he didn't pay his bills he was no longer being supplied with records, and at the time there was some suspicion that he might have been just a long firm. . . . In order for him then to get his records, he started ordering them through this little shop in South Woodford, and it so turned out that this shop in South Woodford was one of my customers, and he went all of a sudden from just ordering records on the basis that you would expect from a little record shop in South Woodford—all of a sudden he was ordering them by the hundred, hundreds and hundreds of records. So I was able to give him credit notes for around £100 a time, so now with one person I'm already getting twice as much as I was getting from all the bits and pieces with all the others. It was great, it was absolutely great.

This went on for about six months. By this time, the company were getting ready to move into their new building. I've got a nice few quid out of all this caper anyway and I was getting sick of the work. I thought, this can't go on for long; it's time to get out. I'll do one more big round of all my customers and then I'll get out. So I put in my notice and went ahead with the plan, and the funny thing was that while I was working out a month's notice . . . the same director . . . pulled me in 'cos he wanted me to start checking out any credit notes valued at £100 or more. In effect, he was setting me on another case, which would be investigating myself. Of course, by then my notice was already in. . . . Left the company, never heard another word about it. Mind you, I've never used them for records. But that was it, yeah, it was great.

But Jock was no longer a professional criminal. The commitment had been slopped out, and he finally succeeded in leading precisely the kind of life that crime was supposed to save him from.

I was lucky because I got a job . . . and your friends and family hadn't given up on you after. They think maybe he's learned his lesson now. Got back together with my girlfriend—she was up the stick and I was about to be a father, so that was a whole different ball game. And actually then I had no other choice than to get on to the commuter train and be a wage slave, on to that selfsame treadmill that I'd always wanted to avoid. And in actual fact that's how I ended up doing another sentence . . . about nine years later. Although you could get work it was difficult to get any sort of quality work, especially with a record behind you.

I found myself doing this job, part of which was looking after the petty cash, which wasn't so petty it was about £1,000. The nature of the job itself was very boring—wouldn't take me more than a day and a half a week to actually do—so I had a lot of spare time. It was quite autonomous in one sense. But I kept thinking, I'm doing this poxy job and at the end of the week I've got about a fiver to myself—this is no good.

So it wasn't long before the hands were going into the petty cash, and I was using that for gambling.

Probably the most remarkable thing about it all was it actually went on for two years before anyone tumbled what was going on. And, interestingly enough, on that occasion, this was working for —— one of the biggest corporations in the world, they've caught me misappropriating £1,000 of their money on the one hand, but at the same time they had a president, president of the corporation in America, who had only been in the job about seven months. It turned out that he was going to get nicked for tax evasion. He hadn't filed in a tax return for five years. So there was me, gambled away £1,000 of their money, call a copper. Before I can say Jack Robinson I'm on remand in Wandsworth, while the president in America is being told 'Very sorry, you're too much of an embarrassment to stay in the job, but here's quarter of a million dollars pay-off.'[1]

Jock was convicted, and as a consequence lost his home and family. After bitter years living on state benefit, he was eventually drawn to academic study, and is committed now to making a living from teaching and studying penal regimes. Starting at square one he has proved to be a quick learner, and has applied his intelligence and considerable energies once again to avoiding a nine-to-five existence.

When I come up here today to do this interview, and I come up on the train and I see all them people, miserable lot, can't even make eye contact most of them. Looking at the adverts four times I think, cor blimey, it's a lovely hot day—I could have been doing that for the last twenty years.

CHOPPING CHARLIE ON THE PORCELAIN, AND TALKING BOLLOCKS WITH BERT THE BUILDER, BALD BERT, AND ALADDIN

It is one o'clock in the morning in the City Arms. Last orders were called two hours ago, when the publican had three people sipping lager amongst the flock wallpaper and soft-porn peanut ads. There are now eighteen customers in the pub, and satellite TV is showing a thriller that broadsheet critics claim has a powerful feminist subtext. However, with the sound turned off, the film acts as little more than an additional source of light, framing the conversations of the all-male clientele, and offering the option of casual visual distraction during spasmodic gaps in the various conversations to which the men turn their attentions.

Some of the men speak loudly, others softly. Outside the alcove everyone is speaking English, while inside they are talking bollocks.

BERT THE BUILDER I tell you, it fucking sounds cold out there.
NICK What?
BERT THE BUILDER You can fucking tell, it sounds fucking cold. Listen. [Quiet.] See?
BRIAN Can't hear a fucking thing.
BERT THE BUILDER That's what I fucking mean—it sounds fucking cold. That's all I'm saying—you can hear it. Listen.

NICK Fuck off [Quiet.]

BERT THE BUILDER Listen, when I was in Gambia it was so hot you could hear everything. Flies and fucking lions and that. The fucking noise, you wouldn't believe it, 'cos it's so hot.

NICK Lions don't fucking live here, do they. You don't get a fucking animal zoo or nothing coming down the street.

BRIAN This time of night the buses have stopped.

PETER But you can get a cab.

BRIAN But not a fucking camel.

PETER Listen. [Rhythmically chinks a glass. Ensemble sing 'Santa Claus is Coming to Town.]

There are six men jammed in and around the corner alcove. Only two of them smoke, but the small circular table is congested testimony to a steady intake of bottled premium lager. Tonight is a regular, unremarkable mid-week rendezvous for a loose collection of men who make most of their money from crime but are committed to leisure. They are marked out from the other late drinkers by the pace and haphazard content of their conversation, and by the frequency which several members of the group visit the toilet, a frequency that contradicts their relatively modest intake of beer.

Fat Bert has been dealing in cocaine for about two years since Peter became unreliable and started demanding payments from people that he had failed to supply. Fat Bert has the shabbiest appearance of anyone in the pub. With his shiny polyester trousers, polyester shirt cutting into his armpits, fading trainers, and more hair in his ears than on his head. Central Casting would typecast him as pub glass-collector rather than a cocaine-dealer. Fat Bert's youth was charactized by violence and later prison. You have to look very closely indeed to discern the pitted crescent of small scars that frame his left eye. Amongst the cheesy texture of his face they appear at first to constitute merely additional blemishes, but it was a sharp instrument rather than poor diet that was responsible for his visage.

Bert chops Charlie on the cold white porcelain of the toilet cistern, and organizes the powder into lines, leaving his company to enjoy it at will. The cubicle is ignored by the remainder of the pub's clientele, and on this particular night Sammy is its most frequent user. He has spent the last two months enjoying the fruits of a burglary of a carpet warehouse. But it was when he succeeded in selling his entire stock within a week that he was awarded the title Aladdin, for making the carpets fly. Although he is only in his early twenties Sammy has proved himself to be a competent thief, but more importantly a highly successful trader. A year earlier Sammy had not been a City Arms regular; now he is snorting coke as part of a discreet urban élite, several of whom are old enough to be his father. He is wearing a well-cut suit of fashionably generous proportions, and his exclusive designer watch is one that will not turn his wrist green. Everyone expects him to be a future money-maker.

Bert the Builder does not build things any more. He used to subcontract as a jobbing builder, but when he reached 30 he retired, claiming that it was a 'young man's game'. By that time he had a long-standing arrangement with a neighbour who was a postman, buying anything from his sack. This was obviously a risky investment, but he survived by selling on cheques or credit cards to Fat Bert, and distributing pirated videos and 'snide' designer clothing. Now in his mid-thirties, he is always to be found immaculately dressed for early summer even in mid-winter. Tonight he wears gold-buckled slip-on shoes and peach-coloured slacks with a red polo shirt under a pink cotton cardigan with white trim. A boxing fan, he is enthusiastic about a forthcoming trip to the States with Brian to watch a world title fight. Brian is one of those people in the pub not smartly dressed, preferring instead his work clothes of slightly baggy denims, track-suit top, and black roll-neck with a golfing logo. His training-shoes are state of the art.

Brian was a useful amateur boxer who loves cocaine. He was the last to arrive at the pub that night after selling tickets for a mediocre derby match between two unsuccessful football teams. I had in the past watched Brian and his colleagues at work. They would arrive at the box-office early and buy a batch of tickets. If the turnstile operators queried why they were not entering the ground they merely replied that they had to meet friends outside. The mark-up appears pretty arbitrary. In one night I observed Brain selling £12 seats for £15 and £18, whatever the immediate market would stand. The fact that the customer could purchase the same ticket for the original price at the box-office was apparently irrelevant. Brian always had 'plenty of money'. Although an eager visitor to Bald Bert's cubicle, Brian was merely being sociable, as he had access to a number of prime sources of cocaine, and had in the recent past retailed amphetamines with his elder brother. Brian worked with a group of men who had close connections with a major football club, and via the club could obtain tickets for the most popular fixtures. Tonight's match had been a mundane, bread-and-butter affair for Brian. The big money came with all-ticket matches when their connections at the club claimed their business perks, and Brian and his colleagues would seek out eager cash buyers.

One of his regular customers was Peter, who would never miss a Cup Final. In fact Peter did not like to miss out on anything. From a family of market traders, Peter had inherited the family business while still in his early twenties. However, the early-morning starts travelling to some damp provincial town interfered with his social life, prompting Peter to hand over the day-to-day running of the business to his younger brother. He married the daughter of a local publican and soon after became involved in a long-running feud with his new in-laws when the police discovered a quantity of stolen TVs in a store-room at the back of the pub. Peter had put them there to cool off, and his father-in-law lost his licence. Consequent police attention lead to Peter's brother-in-law serving a prison sentence and the die was cast.

The resulting feud has now been running for just over twenty years, and erupts spasmodically into bouts of extreme violence between the two tribes, which have often drawn on the resources of some of the most potent criminal families in the neighbourhood. A pub shooting in the early 1980s was, according to official police accounts, drug-related. However, the victim was a nephew of Peter's, and his attackers were close associates of his in-laws. When Peter's family retaliated with the slashing of two men, and a shooting that yielded one relatively minor injury, it was to protect family pride rather than their business interests. Similarly, when Peter's car was burnt out following a dispute with a local thief concerning Peter's alleged failure to fulfil his financial commitment to a consignment of stolen goods, it was to his in-laws that he looked for recompense, for it was they who claimed responsibility. He gained satisfaction with the help of a can of brake fluid, and attacked his father-in-law's car, subsequently receiving a severe beating from a number of men close to the in-laws. Consequently, the separation of business and pleasure in the analysis of violent professional criminal culture can be a fraudulent exercise. It tends to produce one-dimensional portraits that owe more to legalistic diktats and the exigencies of both the criminal justice system and the mass media than the byzantine complexities of contemporary urban cultural forms.

Peter had lived abroad for five years, involved in a time-share business, and it was as a result of this enterprise that he incurred the enduring wrath of Fat Bert. Peter had arranged for Fat Bert and his fiancée to stay in an apartment at a holiday development in which Peter had an interest. However, when he arrived he found that the apartment had been double-booked with a Scottish family. Bert remonstrated with the occupants, a fight broke out, and when he regained consciousness in the bath, he found his fiancée enjoying a drink with her new friends. Fat Bert never forgave Peter, who denied responsibility and refused a refund.

Peter left his wife and two children in a flat above a supermarket in Tenerife, and returned to London to join the late eighties property boom. With the 1990s came the collapse of the property market and Peter's discovery of cocaine, but he became so unreliable that Fat Bert was able to replace him as the neighbourhood white-powder supplier. Peter now lives ten miles away with a woman who works for a PR company, who had given him a lift home after they had both attended a record company launch. The only people willing to listen to coked-up Peter's tales of rock stars, page three models, and celebrity toupees are two men in their early twenties standing at the bar some distance from the alcove, who retain some connection with Fat Bert *et al.* by paying for the rounds of lager that help to fuel the banter. They have dropped into the pub on their way to a night-club. Although they are wearing jeans, they explain that they will bypass the dress code of the club as they are friendly with the bouncers who work the door. They are thieves, there to pay their respects to Peter, whose brother the pony-tailed one had shared a cell with. The previous week both

Pony-tail and his crop-haired mate had been severely reprimanded by the publican for smoking dope, and tonight's flashing of cash is their way of making
amends for an indiscretion, which in the circumstances is something of a mys-
tery which received no explanation other than 'The guv'nor don't like it.'

The last member of the group is Nick, who is a gambler, which is a bit like
saying that Mohammed Ali could box. Nick once stole a car from a car lot and
the next day sold it back to the same dealer. He did it for a bet, but he is also
greedy. When he stole a load of cigarettes and quietly moved them all within
days, he still could not resist the enquiries that continued to come in from
prospective buyers looking for a bargain. He had a complete and regularly
formed pair of ears before he sold the empty cartons to the wrong people, who
knew the difference between right and rip-off. Now his left ear looks like it is
made of plasticine.

When he worked for London Underground Nick was involved in recycling
old tickets, and stole the necessary materials to forge travel passes. He was
arrested for the recycling and sold the forgery materials. He has been dog-racing
tonight and is going straight from the pub to a warehouse near Heathrow that
is storing large quantities of counterfeit perfumes to be merged with the duty-
free trade. Nick is stocking up for Christmas, he has already taken his orders
from local traders, and in the afternoon the horses beckon. Chance holds the
imperative and this time tomorrow Nick could be either rich or asking the
custody sergeant for another blanket.

THE CASUALTY: WAYNE'S WORLD

Wayne used to lurk in the City Arms. He had gone to school with Brian, and
had kept in touch as they had grown up. Wayne liked cocaine a lot. Most
importantly, however, he liked the idea of the cocaine business, for the pharma-
cological and commercial effects seemed so beneficial that it would have been
foolish, almost negligent, to ignore them. However, to the rest of the Wednesday
night group in the City Arms Wayne had become a nuisance, failing to pay for
his share of the coke, and constantly attempting to arrange loans. Eventually he
was informally barred from their group, and for a few weeks hung around on the
periphery hoping to be invited back in, before eventually fading away. Peter was
especially hostile. 'Soapy smelly cunt's a fucking junkie or what? Couldn't have
a toot like anybody else; gets fucking all more, more. But no fucking money.
Fuck him.' But Wayne's story is somewhat more complicated, combining the
magic realism of the late twentieth-century mean streets and the rhetoric of the
catwalk.

I know exactly the day that it really started. Like the day I knew that coke was my real
drug of choice. That's what the fucking social workers and that call it—'drug of choice'—
about right yeah, my drug of choice. I had used it, but always in people's houses or in

the motor before going in a club. Now, you know what it's like when it's new: you have to find out about it and you don't know what it's gonna do, so you are well uptight. And it felt good, bit like you are waiting for something blinding to happen, and you are tense and that. Then after a couple of weeks, it was a Friday and I was out early that night. I scored during the day and I was really up for it, looking forward to a good night out. During the week I met this sort, like a model, nearly as tall as me she was, long black hair.

So this Friday it's the first time I been out with her so I spent all afternoon in the bath, so clean I fucking squeaked. I put this grey herring-bone suit on, no tie but a blue polo shirt, coke in me top pocket, and a fucking great wedge in me bin [pocket]. I had a toot before I gets to the pub and I feel the total fucking business. Everything is like crystal, clear as a bell, but like controlled by me. Then she walks in, and the boozer's only got about twenty people in 'cos its so early, but it went like a fucking tomb, like everything stopped. She walked towards me looking like something out of a fucking advert. And I'm thinking either this gear is fucking wonderful or I'm in love. We have a quick drink and then off we go to this place, well they call it a sort of wine bar but really it's a boozer that's been done up. I had another fucking toot and off we go. Me, I'm a millionaire with Miss World on me arm.

We goes in and 'cos it's so early everybody notices, like turns round and looks. Now there's a group of geezers at the bar, one of them's the landlord, been drinking all afternoon, they think that they are Jack the Lads but I fucking know that I am. So they all look and I make an entrance, sort of stand in the doorway and give it some back. Then as I ordered the drinks I notice that two of the geezers, there's about six of 'em, are still staring at Miss World. Now she's a tall sort, well-dressed, bit of class, and they're pissed, and I know that they are talking about her. But it's my pub now, my night, my bird, it's all crystal, so I smile and offered to buy them all a drink. The geezer with his back to me, turns out it's the landlord, turns round and says something about 'Save your money, son, or this mob are gonna fuck your sort.' Then they all laughed. So it's all right as it's my night and I know I can do anything, so I grab her by the arm and march her out. Then by the door I just pointed to the landlord, smiled, and says 'Don't go away.' I goes outside, give her the keys, little peck on the cheek, and tells her to wait. Then I go fast.

Wayne then gave a highly stylized account of a fight that was partly confirmed to me by one of the customers at the bar, who was an off-duty detective.

It was sweet, so clean, so quick. I walked to the car, got in, and drove off for an Indian. The sort, she weren't too impressed as I remember. Nothing came of it.

Wayne had been a regular user of alcohol since he was about 11, solvents soon after, and cannabis and LSD since the age of 15. Petty theft and vandalism rather than personal violence accompanied his recreational drug use.

Never a fighter, me, you know that. Never bothered. All I ever wanted to do was to get out of my fucking head and avoid going to work. But when the coke thing started it was like I could see a future for myself.

Indeed Wayne's vision of the future is totally wedded to the use and marketing of cocaine. It has provided a dreamlike projection of a clean white world of BMWs and Armani suits. Of crystal sharpness and unrelenting certainty, Wayne's future, if viewed through either nostril, is assured, both spiritually and economically.

His chronic lateness in arriving for appointments is due to his involvement in a 'little', 'big', or 'fucking blinding' deal, depending on how late he is. His ability to cope with situations over which he has no control depends on his sense of well-being, which in turn is determined by his intake of cocaine. Most importantly, however, Wayne's self-image as a yuppie gangster, dealing in coke and controlling his environment through his own use of the drug, is somewhat at odds with the spotty, slightly dishevelled figure in the saloon bar of the City Arms. Wayne's skin is at once acne-scarred and semi-transparent, his suit is off-the-peg, and the jacket appears to contain someone else's shoulders, with crinkled grooves on the padding. His shoes are cheap and his shirts polyester–cotton mix. He is unconvincing. On a warm day, Wayne will smell.

About six months after his adoption of cocaine as a life-force, he started telling anyone who would listen that he had bought a shotgun, and at first his boasts were ignored. He claimed that 'I fired it once down by the canal where they go ratting—that was just to make sure it worked.' A few rumours began to circulate that Wayne had robbed an all-night garage, but they were discounted as 'junkie talk'. By now it was common knowledge that he was using crack and he stopped hanging around the City Arms, but in his absence the rumours compounded into something resembling a criminal reputation. When Wayne's flatmate was arrested for armed robbery it became apparent that robbery had become part of his fantasy life-style. His flatmate was eventually convicted of robbing shops and off licences. Meanwhile Wayne was working alone for barely sufficient return to finance his own habit. When the police visited his flat following a neighbour's complaints of a noisy argument, he had two rocks of crack in his pocket and a vintage air-rifle under his bed. Wayne was released from prison, and while this book was being written up, died of pneumonia after apparently living rough on the streets for a couple of months.

COKE NOT COAL

This is an urban élite at play. Their working lives driven by a narcissistic desire to squeeze the last drop of pleasure from fruit that they have always known was rotten. Life is a party, the sort of party where you gatecrash and then shit in the bath. A piss-up in a brewery, a noonday plunge into a warm bath of midnight. There must always be a buzz from wheeling and dealing or staying sharp to the last gram. Cash on the hip and plenty of lip.

Two weeks later and it's two thirty in the morning. As Nick arrives, a young man, possibly still of school age, bursts into the pub. He is wearing a filthy shell suit and on his back he carries a sack of coal. He is bent double under the weight and the pub is silent. The landlord explains apologetically to the boy that the pub is 'all gas', and the boy staggers silently out. As he leaves, a small dog comes into the pub and trots inquisitively around the chairs and tables before pausing in front of the alcove. Bert the Builder catches the dog's eye, then stares at the door. 'Listen, you can hear how fucking cold it is.'

Appendix. Cell Mates

That was totally amazing. In Wandsworth on remand, you're in a cell twenty-three hours a day. One evening when they've opened us up for the evening, tea and bun or whatever it is, at the same time as the new receptions were coming in, I've seen a face that I recognized and given him a tug and said 'I know you from somewhere. Where do you live?' And he said 'Hounslow'. I've never been to Hounslow. I live in Ilford. He'd never been to Ilford. So the next logical thing is, well, I must have seen you inside. And sure enough it turned out we had shared a cell in Wormwood Scrubs nine years earlier, and he was in on that occasion for taking and driving away, and it turned out he was in this time for stealing a car. He'd been in various times in the intermediate nine years, always with car-related stuff. Anyway, that was that and we were back in our cells again. So I was thinking about, 'cor blimey, talk about small world.

The very next morning, gone downstairs to get breakfast, as I'm holding my mug out while the geezer's slopping some tea into it he says to me 'It's a long time since I've seen you in Wormwood Scrubs.' I looked round. This was the feller who came into the cell after the bloke I'd met the night before had moved out, again nine years previous. Exactly the same thing. He was in for taking and driving away, and he'd been in more times than you care to remember in the intermediate nine years, always taking and driving away . . . Gobsmacked. I cannot tell you how much of a gobsmacker that was. Says a lot about, I guess, the prison system. And again, it makes you think about yourself. You think, what am I doing here? What sort of a chump am I to be caught up in this?

Jock lost everything this time, including his family. Bitter with the way in which the criminal justice system had responded to his case, he started to read law and found what he maintains to this day was a discrepancy in his treatment.

I was charged under the Theft Act, and in order for a successful conviction under the Theft Act there are five elements that have to be satisfied, and one of them is the accused must have the intention to permanently deprive the owner of their property. Now, it was never my intention to permanently deprive. I'd been using their money for two years and had always, if anything had gone wrong, it was always rebunged. I borrowed money from the bank or whatever. So had I known this, I would have actually gone to court and pleaded not guilty, but because of the nature of the legal system . . .

I've seen the Duty Solicitor, who's an absolute clown, for about two minutes. Throughout the whole thing I've remained in ignorance of this clause of the Theft Act that I think would have got me off, and instead of that I end up getting nine months. As far as I was concerned, that wasn't justice. That was the end of family life and all the rest of it.

The only thing that stopped Jock from returning to full-time crime was fear of prison.

Interestingly enough, when I got out on that occasion, that was as close as I'd ever been from the days when I was a professional criminal to thinking about going back to it, because I felt as though I'd been the victim of rough justice. I wasn't interested in working, I knew I wouldn't get any sort of a job or anything like that. For a long time I was seriously considering about getting back at it, because although technically I'd broken the law the second time, that had nothing to do with criminal intent; it wasn't because I wanted to be a criminal or was doing it to be a criminal.

But the threat of prison was sufficient to deter Jock from returning to crime. Yet despite his new-found career he fights shy of making any sanctimonious claims that he is reformed.

No, you can't help it. Every time I go into a bank it brings back memories and I think of things that have happened on previous occasions when I've been in. And you do, there's a sort of knee-jerk response that you look around at things like that. But what has tickled me over perhaps the last ten years or so, I'm thinking all those years ago I used to go in, and I'm thinking of ways that you could rob them . . . and fraud them or whatever, and yet the last ten years it seems to me all you've got to do is go and ask them. They can't wait to give it to you nowadays. I can't understand actually why anyone wants to go in and rob them when they're so eager to give it to you. You don't have to forge anything. Makes you think if the game goes rotten one of these days, just go into as many banks as you can and say, well how much will you lend me, and then take it all, and off you go to the Caribbean. (Laughs.)

8
Criminal Life

> Criminal life is, thus, a succession of deals. The average wiseguy has, typically, four or five deals in the air at any one time. They are partnerships, in varying combinations, that he has put together with his own immediate contacts, with the members of other criminal rings, and from time to time, with a recruit from the straight world—a truck driver, perhaps, who is willing to look the other way when his load gets hijacked. It is a matter of individual enterprise, and the share out at the end of it—payday—is the measure of how successful any particular deal has been.
>
> (R. Lacey, *Little Man*)

It is apparent that the practice of professional criminals is somewhat contrary to the exploits of the romantic outlaws of classic gangster fiction, who belong to an occupationally cohesive group whose practice mirrors that of the legitimate order.[1] There is no mirror image: it is the same business, albeit with a certain visceral edge one is unlikely to find in even the most aggressive firm of chartered accountants.

Unlike Sutherland's professional,[2] who operated within the boundaries of a well-defined maverick subculture, the enacted environments of professional criminality are not homogeneous. Like the markets that they seek to manipulate and plunder, these environments embrace infinite variations, and are largely indistinguishable from the arenas that facilitate legitimate entrepreneurial pursuits. These arenas support instrumental networks that function as enabling environments for a plethora of money-making opportunities, some of which will be either partly or wholly criminal. The markets themselves will shape the entrepreneurial options that are available within any given arena.[3]

PLACES

The emergence of the market-place as the crucial dynamic within contemporary society stresses the redundancy of any analysis of serious crime that is restricted to the parameters of traditional neighbourhoods. For unlike traditional localized criminal organizations, with their adherence to the formal relations inherited and adapted from the indigenous socio-economic sphere,[4] the contemporary serious crime community is the 'arch enemy of uniformity'.[5] Indeed the ethos of entrepreneurship that underpins all activity within the post-traditional market-place thrives upon variety and diversification.[6]

Within the maelstrom of change that has affected the modern urban land-scape, the market provides an integration of the prospect of autonomous action and the seductive illusion of certainty.[7] As Chapter 1 clearly indicates, the decline and in some cases destruction of key criminal crafts and trades has resulted in an emphasis upon 'New technical, social, psychological and existential skills . . . practicable only in conjunction with marketable commodities'.[8] This is particularly apparent from the various narratives in Chapters 6 and 7, which indicate the serious-crime community's accelerating dependency upon entrepreneurial performance in the drug trade and related action, such as the production and supply of counterfeit goods, which marks the passing of those skills that 'do not entail the use of marketable commodities; the more complete the destruction, the more necessary become new skills which point organically to market supplied implements'.[9]

Serious criminality involves competent engagement with both legal and illegal markets, and an understanding of how these markets function is necessary for the exercise of power. In the case of working-class entrepreneurship, the exercise of power is often inextricably bonded to violence or potential for violence. In this respect crime as an integral component of working-class entrepreneurial action represents a 'gendered life course'[10] *par excellence*.

TROUBLE AT MILL

Definitions of competent practice are of course negotiated within specific indigenous cultures, which in turn have been created as communal responses to the demands of local economies and will be in a constant state of flux.[11] Craft skills and traditional trades which have been crucial in defining and shaping images of masculinity may no longer be available to create viable gendered careers for men.[12] In addition, unskilled employment opportunities have declined, along with the patriarchal base upon which recruitment, work practices, and neighbourhood ecology were grounded.[13] Crime can be seen as a way of rebuilding this patriarchal base on the original site and with many of the traditional ingredients. Crime, like the bulk of activities that are integral to both traditional and post-traditional societies, is a boys' game, and, like most boys' games, it is exclusive, heavily coded, and contains an essential tension between team spirit and individual expression.

Working-class communities often cling to a communal imagery that is reliant upon highly specialized craft competencies and complementary elements of muscular signifiers in order to define essences perceived as essential for the maintenance of internal hierarchies. Nevertheless, as these essences lose their transformative capacity, and are identified as economically redundant, any traditional strategy that retains market potential becomes elevated to the forefront of the practical consciousness of agents and to the cutting edge of entrepreneurial strategy.[14]

The durability of these markets will be limited by the local opportunities that survive in the form of the indigenous debris of industrial society.[15] Further, the ability of individuals to exploit these remnants will often depend upon the cultural inheritance that has been forged in the local economy. Therefore, competencies within the market-place are likely to coincide due to the manner in which working-class male culture is shaped by the nature of the local formal and informal economies. The residue of traditional masculine working-class culture, the potential for violence and instrumental physicality that remains from industrial domestic and employment cultures, once it is divested of the potential for communal action via collective responsibility, is ideally situated for engagement with serious crime.

Traditional criminal networks, like traditional cultures based upon manufacturing industries, are susceptible to the tides of change, and have been 'lifted out' of their local contexts, and 're-articulated across time-space'.[16] For Nissan in Sunderland, and Kentucky Fried Chicken in Cardiff, read cocaine in London and cannabis in Glasgow. The subsequent reproduction of traditional strategies from within the agency of the market suggests that the structural elements that secure and shape the various commercial practices that go to make up the market's enacted environment are at some point transformed into enabling devices.

The emergent 'dialectic of control'[17] reproduces and exaggerates those aspects of traditional working-class culture that have some viability, no matter how ambiguous its application. These 'inductive inferences from past trends, or from past experience [are] believed in some way to be dependable for the present'.[18] Traditional images of masculinity, along with potential for violence played out from within networks based upon the family and their proximity to active markets, constitute such inductive inferences, and are crucial aspects of working-class culture that emerge as enabling strategies, coherent within both the market-place and the moral economy of commercial practice.[19] 'These networks will in turn inform the market place but not organise it; the networks imbue action with a significance that is common to individuals engaging in many types of illicit activity . . . and constitute what is often labelled as "the underworld".'[20]

THE UNDERWORLD

> The world was different then. People believed in God, and children died at early ages of the fever and tuberculosis. Saints and angels walked in gardens.
>
> (Oscar Hijuelos, *Our House in the Last World*)

One of the most powerful of these inductive inferences, one which has no obvious instrumental function, is the codification of professional criminal culture, an essential segment of the rhetoric of the serious-crime community referred to in the Introduction. Criminal biographies feature references to these inferences usually as a way of explaining generational shifts in moral aptitude.[21]

The most forceful claim upon the primacy of these inferences in made by Frank Fraser, whose career spans the immediate pre-war and entire post-war period to date, and whose criminality is closely tied to an overt almost Samurai vindication of violent action in pursuit of inverted honour.[22] For instance, in the mid-1960s while enjoying his long-standing alliance with the Richardson Brothers, Fraser received a veiled threat from Eric Mason, an associate of the rival Kray firm. Fraser explained his reaction to this insult to his finely honed sensibilities:

> he was bang out of order. You can't go around saying things like that and not expecting anything to happen. I know it sounds if it was a bit rough, the punishment, but it wasn't excessive although it might sound it to people who didn't understand the rules.[23]

Eric Mason describes the extent of Fraser's slap on the wrist:

> I saw the axe coming down once and put my hand up to shield my head. The blow pinned my hand to my skull. It was then that I realised that I had serious injuries as I couldn't move parts of my body. . . . I had over thirty serious injuries, three fractures to my skull and over three hundred stitches in various parts of my body.[24]

As Fraser explains, 'As I say Eric wasn't a bad fellow, but that particular night he was bang out of order'.[25]

Being 'bang out of order', showing disrespect for the rules, collaborating with police, or breaking some arcane dress code,[26] can invoke dire consequences.[27] The teasing-out and reinvention of these tried and tested strategies, the disparate range of skills and marketing devices which constitute 'Systems of accumulated expertise',[28] is vital, particularly within an environment that can alter so radically, so quickly. Inductive inferences allow the individual 'Within the limits permitted by the culture to define, for himself somewhat new patterns suggested by the variation among the old ones'.[29]

Consequently, the periodic re-emergence of sacred myths related to traditional strategies and iconic individuals serves to maintain a sense of continuity. This is what Dick Pooley[30] consistently referred to as 'the criminal fraternity', a microcosm of occupationally distinct individuals defined by their persistent and competent involvement in criminal activities for monetary gain. Despite their overwhelming incoherence in relation to the successful completion of contemporary serious crime, which, as Chapters 3, 4, and 5 suggest, involves the engagement of legitimate entrepreneurial strategies, the periodic resurrection of crucial aspects of the code creates a vision of what, in the face of such radical alterations to both the legal and illegal base (which despite its enhancement of pecuniary opportunities is often disorientating), can only be an imaginary community that leans heavily upon an invented tradition.[31] The result is a 'retrospective unity',[32] that manifests itself in the present as a cosy, essentially homogeneous sphere of activity that aspires to ideals or 'a constantly receding horizon'[33] of communal underworld fantasy. This fantasy is, as Lacey notes, highly functional, for it is 'an integral element of how organised crime is experienced, perceived, and reported. Many of the criminals themselves are fantasists.'[34]

The underworld fantasy enables the professional criminal in times of crisis to conjure some order from the imaginary community and inject it into a life-world that is prone to chaotic, seemingly incoherent interludes. It is from a combination of these archaeological excursions and regular engagements with the enacted environments of contemporary serious criminality that professional criminals appropriate their identities.

However, the mobile telephones, connections across continents, visits to Amsterdam, and the prospect, if it 'all comes on top', of going missing in Brazil instead of your uncle's caravan in Frinton, removes the emphasis from these essential interactions that were implicit to the criminal fraternity, and virtually eliminates not only much of the trust upon which traditional criminal networks were grounded, but also the risk, the management of which created one of the most revered measures of competency within narratives of the old underworld. The resultant temporary alignments of criminal personnel lean heavily upon an ethos of instrumental decision-making that is in itself the antithesis of what Frank Fraser and a small group of underworld icons has represented for nearly half a century.

Yet it is vital that these eternal recurrences of codified underworld themes should not be ignored completely, for the rhetoric of élite professionalism[35] constitutes a quest for order[36] that is a direct response to the essential ambiguity of contemporary serious crime. The Krays, the Richardsons, Frank Fraser, Billy Hill, and Derby Sabini may now seem as dated as their tailoring, but it is not merely their obvious regard for traditional hand-stitching that remains relevant. For their most important function is that of providing cultural chaperons for contemporary entrepreneurial criminals, informing their integrity and providing important reference-points that relate to a heavily mythological past that in retrospect appears highly stylized, rigidly structured, and imbued with chivalrous intent. Such Arthurian pretensions were of course misplaced in the underworld heyday of the mid-1960s,[37] but none the less afford some clues to an appropriate and culturally cogent identity, particularly for those criminals who, while committed to serious crime, remain rooted either literally or metaphorically in traditional locations and in traditional practices.[38]

This reconstitution of continuities made familiar by the repetitive translation of the conventions and procedures of key iconic individuals, enables the construction of enduring monuments to obscure and redundant practices. They become safe objects without context, devoid of threat, therefore defining a set of social relations that can only be located contemporaneously within the parameters of a theme park. As a consequence, the common cultural perception of Britain's underworld is over a quarter of a century old with a razor wound under its left eye, never grasses, and was banged up behind a vacuum-sealed time-lock before flared trousers made the chain stores.

What is normally referred to as the underworld relates to a specific section of the West End of London, Soho, at a specific time, late 1930s to early 1970s. It also refers to a specific set of economic relations surrounding gaming- and drinking-clubs. This was the context within which criminals from well-established enclaves in north, south, east, and west London, along with a sprinkling of Italians and Maltese, formed a particularly vivid mosaic of business and pleasure.[39] Launched by the outbreak of the Second World War, and sunk by a combination of police corruption, police action, and gentrification, the British underworld is so restricted by time and space as to make the concept irrelevant now, a 'Messianic time'[40] of sacred myth that has parallels with rightist golden-age scenarios that pine for 'traditional' standards of law and order. However, as time passes, and ancient legends become little more than a signed special edition,[41] the underworld's potency is diminished, carrying clout from beyond the grave only to fuel our suspicions that '"somewhere," "somebody" is pulling all the complicated strings to which the world dances'.[42]

Yet we are concerned here with more than metaphysical issues, for the problem of the underworld is located not so much in the practice of serious crime, with its frauds, scams, and trade-offs sitting side by side with more visceral enterprise, but with the legitimizing and enabling rhetorics of entrepreneurship that have evolved from the very society that the legend of the underworld was constructed to oppose.[43] Consequently, the problem is not one of exclusion, the self-containment of an élite practice, but of inclusion of the individuals and practices within the entire 'spectrum of legitimacy';[44] accountants, businessmen, and anyone with the capital for a return trip to Amsterdam and sufficient cash to invest in a stash.

Contemporary professional criminals are faced with roaming a territory of the mundane that is largely indistinct from that occupied by civilians. Yet their distinct identities cannot be totally denied by the ambivalence that is a by-product of enterprise culture and other aspects of the post-traditional order. For this ambivalence also creates the possibilities of new identities forged as a result of engagement with, but most importantly the management and manipulation of, opportunities that have their origins in global as opposed to purely local markets. For at the intersection of the old neighbourhood and the new market, money is made at a distance several steps removed from the point of production and with a confrontational potential as discreet as a bailiff's business card. Contemporary serious-crime groups differ from all preceding forms of criminality 'in respect of their dynamism, the degree to which they undercut traditional habits and customs, and their global impact'.[45]

As Block has noted, professional criminals should be seen 'as fluid sets of mobile marauders in the urban landscape alert to institutional weakness in both legitimate and illegitimate spheres'.[46] These spheres are, as Chaney has suggested, intrinsically malleable and are not located in fixed terrain,[47] as they are manifested as both local and global networks of opportunity and feature ill-defined contours that must encapsulate the inheritance of locales steeped in traditional notions of criminogenic trajectories, while engaging with contemporaneous variations upon themes established by the precedents of indigenous markets. The manner in which essential essences of traditional criminal organizations are 'transmuted'[48] suggests that primacy will always be afforded to those groups who are able to retain a sense of historical perspective and apply pertinent inductive inferences to activities that have yet to be fully established in our society's cultural imagination as any more than variations on normative commercial themes.[49]

However, as locally based villains increasingly afford primacy to engagements with a multiplicity of drug markets, the territory that defined their very existence is being broken down, and the culture of serious crime becomes removed from the territory that spawned its most prominent practitioners and their elementary forms of organization.[50] As the globalization of legitimate markets have contributed to the erosion of traditional cultures, so drugs and the subsequent global drug markets that have evolved since the 1970s have contrived to erode the links between traditional criminal territories and the criminal cultures that they spawn. The contemporary illegal market mirrors its legitimate counterpart in that it is typified by the dialectic between the local and the global,[51] and the ensuing enacted environment within which entrepreneurial personnel engage with the market in a variety of culturally specific forms is too complex for the largely tautological term 'organized crime'.[52]

BACK SPACES

This complexity does not, however, negate the primacy of the locally based 'firm', for changes to both the socio-economic conditions and the subsequent enacted environments that nurture professional criminals are enduring features of modern societies. However, theirs is a rich lineage stretching back to times when being described as 'the governor of the manor' meant something more than having your own stool in the saloon bar of the Dog and Bastard. Despite the constant fluctuation that contemporary serious criminality endures, long-established patterns of conflict and accommodation pertain.

For instance, the end of feudalism not only marked the redefinition of economic relations, it also heralded the beginnings of urbanization, and it is during this period that we can note the evolution of an identifiable body of individuals whose identities were inextricably bonded to the practice of making money from crime via a commitment that extended beyond the requirements of subsistence.[53] A good example can be located in the new urban demand for meat derived from game, a demand that could not be met by the legitimate sources of these immature markets. Poachers turned professional, and competent operatives committed themselves full-time to market engagement.[54] By the eighteenth century, professional crime had established itself as a predominantly urban phenomenon situated next to the most affluent areas where the demand for goods was highest[55] and the regimentation of the emerging working class was at its most ineffective.[56]

The technological advances and propensity to document contemporaneous social forms that accompanied urbanization yielded accounts that we can use to reach a better understanding of early professional crime. For instance, Rawlings has reproduced a selection of popular pamphlets that provide an at times ambiguous flavour of contemporary accounts of professional criminality. The brief biography of Mary Young gives an outline of the background, skills, and culture of committed eighteenth-century criminals, and suggests a level of organization that is structured around the specific requirements of their criminal trades.[57]

The journalists christened by Downes and Rock as the 'shadow criminologists'[58] ventured boldly amongst London's emergent working class, and succeeded in situating crime within a cultural and geographical framework of self-employment and casual work that, far from signalling its opposition to the prevailing order, was in harmony with the dominant commercial ethic of the age.[59] These writers acknowledged that crime was an essential facet of urban life, intrinsic to the evolution of the city, with elements of structure and organization, and most importantly with a template located not in the underworld, but within the normative economic relations of the overworld.

In turn, the areas in which this deviance was concentrated became highly functional to the evolving city, for, as Rock has noted, 'possibilities of random and unintended confrontation with deviants are considerably reduced'.[60] Further, these emergent deviant enclaves created enabling spaces which were in themselves 'a frame of reference for actions'.[61]

The emergence of these 'alternative geographies'[62] was crucial for the symbolic, yet enduring location of social organizations that enabled negotiated and *ad hoc* engagements with variations on normative forms of enterprise.[63] These 'manors' could then be conquered, and defended. They could be launched into conflicts that would endure for generations, and exploit the indigenous resources by making special claims upon the area's commercial, manufacturing, and leisure base. They served to spawn various enterprises which in turn reinforced a local order built upon a solid foundation of independence, autonomy, and tough masculinity. As crucial agents of this indigenous local order, professional criminals are traditionally firmly situated within geographical and economic parameters, which in turn stress the primacy of the culture's key focal concerns: trouble, toughness, smartness, excitement, and autonomy.[64]

As these manors became, with the diversification of the legitimate workforce, more heterogeneous, the legal market-place provided non-criminal identities to rival the pervasive deviant. Yet there remained a 'reversible transfer of moral substance'[65] between professional criminals and their communities. As this book indicates, despite the massive disruption that has taken place within society, the primary unit of organization of serious criminality to which professional criminals adhere is a constantly mutating network of entrepreneurial arrangements. At the heart, or 'ground zero', of such networks exist traditional 'neighbourhood firms'[66] based on familial and highly localized allegiances. It is within such environments that 'the business of crime is planned, contacts are made, some crimes are carried out, the fruits of crime are often enjoyed, and the methodologies for the integration of organised criminals into civil society are established'.[67]

NEW PLACES

The manufacture and trade in universal consumer and cultural products does not completely destroy the link between culture and territory. 'Disorganised capitalism'[68] has fragmented cultural desires and placed a great emphasis upon highly localized units of provision for what Hirsch has identified as a trend for 'niche' or 'positional' goods.[69] 'In other words there may be a renaissance of the small business emanating from the new culture of "Post-modernism" located within this recently emerged "disorganised" phase of capitalism.'[70]

Key segments of the global drug trade are articulated within a highly local context of territorially based dealing networks,[71] and although some traditional neighbourhood firms will be able to adapt to the unique demands of this new market, others will have to mutate, compete, or rot on the vine as new innovative groups, along with the occasionally fresh entrepreneurial arenas in which some commodities are traded and consumed, serve to redefine the parameters of criminal territories.[72] Localities and dependent identities are therefore reinvented in the context of global markets[73] or adapted to a more malleable indigenous form appropriate to local precedent.

The transformative capacity of the cultural and economic power that constitutes professional criminality is ideally suited to the incessant mediations and renegotiations that co-ordinate relations between both individuals and groups,[74] and duplicate themselves in the form of continually mutating social systems of culturally indeterminable origins and multifarious economic destinations. The rhetoric of enterprise culture has enabled the extraction of any irony from the professional criminal's claim on the status of businessman. When the Krays and others stated that they were not villains but businessmen, there was a *frisson* of excitement, of curiosity, and ultimately expectation that, in the final act, the commercial front would be spectacularly exposed by some outrageous act of apparently irrational savagery.

However, as Chambliss has stressed, 'crime . . . takes its character from the economic institutions that exist at a particular point in time',[75] and contemporary narratives are no longer required to induce apocalyptic denouements to scripts that are located within the post-traditional order. Professional crime has moved

from an occupational foundation of neighbourhood-orientated extortion and in-
dividualistic craft-based larcenies towards an entrepreneurial trading culture driven
by highly localized interpretations of global markets. Within these markets risk
has been reduced by the increasingly impersonal nature of criminal interactions,
the effects of technological innovation, and the subsequent flexibility, both situ-
ationally and ideologically, with which operatives engage with markets.

The emphasis on non-specialization referred to in preceding chapters and
confirmed in a variety of publications[76] suggests that many criminals will not
possess a sharply focused occupational identity. Their identities are shaped by
the relationships that they make as a result of interacting with the money economy.
They are economic actors functioning within a culture of exchange that has not
designated to them a master status that discriminates between the legal and the
illegal. They operate, as we can observe from Chapters 4, 5, and 6, in 'networks
within networks, cross-cutting networks, and even contradictory associations
between networks'.[77] These configurations of networks cannot be abstracted from
the interactions that are negotiated within them.[78] For without a rigid hierarch-
ical base to structure serious criminal action, without 'the big conspiracy, the
Organisation',[79] a concept that will 'inevitably produce a static, incomplete, and
somewhat ahistorical representation of organised crime',[80] we are left with interactions that are co-ordinated in an infinite number of variations which relate
most pertinently to the form of criminal activity in question.[81] The associations
of these networks to specific locales, or territories, is recognition of the inheritance of deviant identities that provides the springboard for innovative market
activity.[82] Further, the clusters of social relations that constitute these networks
are embedded in shared assumptions about the meaning of deviant action, and
this action in itself is liable to interpretive debate.

FUN AND MONEY: LET'S GET LOST

Variations both in markets and in social interactions within often *ad hoc* networks
with a powerful sense of history are apparent throughout this book. Many of the
criminals featured, in particular those in Chapter 7, were driven wholly or partly
by a sense of hedonistic destiny. The life-worlds of contemporary professional
criminals will vary in accord with their practice and chosen spheres of enterprise, for professional criminality does not offer a self-contained economic and
cultural space within which practitioners survive and prosper according to some
heavily coded formula that precisely parallels the normative order. For although
economic rationality is one of the central themes of this book, a significant
group of committed professional criminals are stubbornly and consistently re-
sistant to 'subsystems of purposive rational action'.[83]

For these individuals 'Life is lived without a safety net';[84] they are motivated
by an explicitly hedonistic drive that is summed up by Shover and Honaker as

'life as a party'.[85] Crime funds their life-style, and their life-style is both criminal and dedicated to variations on the high life. 'Earning and burning money'[86] authenticates the outlaw status of this type of criminal and stands in stark contrast to the criminal entrepreneur with his overt commercial rhetoric and quasi-corporate practices.[87]

Allusions to commercial practices are convenient shorthand when justificatory rhetoric is required. This rhetoric is especially attractive to non-criminal audiences as it drips with irony and is wholly appropriate within the broader context of the enterprise culture that has pervaded Anglo-American culture since the early 1980s. However, 'professional', 'business', and 'accounting' metaphors[88] are over-simplistic interpretive devices, denying the range of hedonistic possibilities that are apparent in the various niches and alcoves within which committed serious criminals ply their trades and spend their money.[89]

The hedonistic strand to serious criminality reflects a division of labour that is rooted firmly in traditional practices and traditional proletarian notions of leisure and pleasure. What emerges is a cultural identity that is defined by a commitment both to conspicuous consumption and to the criminal action that funds it. The professional criminal sums it up: 'well I'm a natural. I mean, I am a natural. I, I love the high life. I love the . . . going out to wine and dine, the fucking champagne and the birds, and living it up and first class on the airplanes. Champagne fucking Charlie. You know. Ducking and diving and, you know wining and dining.'[90] These criminals are also often more prone to risk-taking than their more business-like colleagues and 'the threat of chaos is ubiquitous in the life of illicit action. . . . There is the constant threat that the criminal justice system will suddenly wrench control of one's life.'[91]

As a number of writers have indicated, when life is a party, the possible consequences of criminal action are seldom prominent considerations.[92] In this respect they show similar attitudes to risk management as members of more conventional occupational groups. 'Just as bricklayers, for example, do not visualise graphically or deliberate over the bodily carnage that could follow from a collapsed scaffold, many thieves apparently do not dwell at length on the chaos of arrest or the pains of imprisonment. As one of our subjects put it, "you think about going to prison like you think about dying, you know".'[93]

Not only does the straight world not offer them the same financial rewards as the criminal life, it also does not offer the same *frisson* of excitement and exclusivity, as they share with their peers the ambience of 'spontaneity, autonomy, independence and resourcefulness'[94] that constitutes their outlaw status. They have no pretensions towards legitimacy, and there is little ambiguity concerning their life-style. When all is right in their world they stand out from the majority of citizens, who are a 'greedy ignorant mob of mug punters, simply asking to be taken'.[95] They consider that they have seen through the system—they are above the piffling mundanities of everyday society and stand apart from its petty aspirations.

Drug-dealer and convicted murderer and armed robber Robby Wideman explains:

Straight people don't understand. I mean, they think dudes is after the things straight people got. It ain't that at all. People in the life ain't looking for no home and grass in the yard and shit like that. We the show people. The glamour people. Come on the set with the finest car, the finest woman, the finest wines. Hear people talking about you. Hear the bar get quiet when you walk in the door. Throw down a yard and tell everybody drink up. . . . You make something out of nothing.[96]

As is clear from a consideration of the hedonists of Chapter 7, the serious-crime community has the ability to accommodate non-instrumental life-style practitioners. Further, this accommodation is crucial for the maintenance of occupational hierarchies, and the dominance of the drug trade in particular enables a hedonistic engagement with the market-place that serves as an attractive option for anyone seeking to make money from their hobby, or to exploit age-specific market niches. As the references to the overlap with football and dance cultures suggest, it is not necessary for the youth of any one generation to serve an apprenticeship with the professional villains of the parent culture. Indeed, both the 'apprenticeship' of Dick Pooley[97] and the 'culture' of Jock,[98] which are also alluded to by Robin,[99] have given way to innovative strategies that are directly related to the essential contradiction between work and leisure.[100]

The identities of the inhabitants of Chapters 6 and 7 are irrevocably bonded to the pursuit of good times and/or the exploitation of the market opportunities that are afforded to them by their demographic location within the sphere of leisure. Drink, drugs, gambling, etc. require financing as well as offering arenas of opportunity. As Lefebvre notes, 'Thus leisure enters into the division of social labour.'[101]

What is being suggested, therefore, is that as within legitimate networks of economic activity, the gap between instrumental and non-instrumental decision-making is far from clear-cut.[102] The construction of ambiguity is a powerful tool of all professional criminals and is apparent in the duality of the criminal-businessman identity.[103] However, it is also a crucial device in structuring the identities of those practitioners engaging with local leisure markets[104] for whom the apparent ambivalence between hedonism and 'pure' economic engagement can seal the instrumental properties of professional criminality within identifiable networks of deviant action. The relatively fragmented narratives (compared to the traditional models consisting of Messrs Fraser, Kray, Richardson, *et al.*) that make up the personnel rosters of these networks serve as contingencies for markets that generate fragmentation and no longer require the cloak of corporatism to lend an artificial sense of order to transitory, disordered practices. The result is, ironically, a far more potent marketing arrangement that is not hamstrung by arcane practices and their attendant folk memories, nor by the tribal sensibilities of previous eras. As Bauman has noted, 'The more secure the fragmentation, the more desultory and less controllable the resulting chaos.'[105]

Most of the criminals in this book stressed that they get a lot of pleasure from their work. Their generally humble beginnings informed them of what prospects were in store for them, and crime offered not just an alternative economic trajectory, or, as I have suggested above, a pleasanter life-style than one spent in mundane occupations or surviving on welfare. They also, particularly early on in their careers, before, as Jock suggests,[106] deviance in itself starts to replicate the drudgery of work, are exhilarated by their practice; they get a 'buzz'[107] that is based upon an explicit recognition of the oppositional inferences of their deviance.[108] Despite being inspired by the resultant chaos, competent deviants can find themselves drawn ironically to engagements with markets that demand disciplined responses from individuals whose very identities are inspired by disorder.

THE POINT OF CONSUMPTION

The drug business requires personnel to be conversant with the culture of the market at the cutting edge, which, particularly in the case of amphetamines and amphetamine-based products, is manifested at the point of consumption. The clubs and pubs of our inner cities have been turned into bazaars by the demand for recreational drugs, and the ability to perform competently within these often highly stylized arenas is a crucial and highly rated, if unarticulated, characteristic amongst both buyers and sellers. Personnel operating at the point of consumption will inevitably display a cultural competence that enables total engagement with their designated commercial environment.

The overt consumption of drugs in and around this environment is a crucial measure of competent performance, and marks the symbiotic relationship between buyers, and sellers, within commercially bounded territories. However, this can only pertain to those substances that enhance trading. Dealers in hallucinogens who enjoy the product while conducting business are obviously operating at a disadvantage, while amphetamines, and more specifically cocaine, offer a perfect commodity with which to straddle the thin divide between work times and good times. The cultural perception of cocaine is that of an enhancer of predatory business acumen. With the cold focus that the drug is perceived to effect, its price and method of delivery, cocaine is an ideal substance with which to embellish both business and pleasure, an elixir of subterranean urban life that turns money into the most ideal attitude of white-light street wisdom.

Leisure outlets such as pubs and clubs provide an arena for these cold performances of mannered intensity. Community allegiances and day-time identities are checked in at the door by these volunteers for anonymous celebrity, a celebrity that is bought from men with pissholes for eyes and a certain rigidity around the neck and jaw-line that suggests imminent combustion. It is exciting, dangerous, moving drugs at street level, and the occasional taste of the good stuff paces the movement of the retail grade that is kept in the inside pocket. Reactions need to be sharp and regularly pampered by surges of adrenalin and the promise of money. Consequently, any enhanced sensitivity to threats or to fluctuations in the enacted market-place will be highly prized by operators seeking to boost pleasure and profit.

Some of these environments are relatively benign, and trade is conducted in an atmosphere of relaxed enterprise, where an air of familiarity cushions the gap between buyer and seller.[109] In these environments a lack of market competition makes it possible for customers to feel that they can achieve a level of intimacy with their supplier. Clubs like Sounds are typically benign, yet undeniably wired: bulwarks of the new understated cocaine-inspired moral economy of the logo-free nineties. The discreet façade of the club is sufficiently low-key to deter the Kevins and Tracys, and within the shabby interior new customers have to work extremely hard to discern that the cut of the suit, the label on the bottle, and the quality of the cocaine are the best and not 'snides', counterfeit copies of a contrary, more up-market reality. Regulars don't bother checking; they take the exclusiveness of anonymity for granted; it's built in to the price.

The dealing, like the stitching around the lapels, is discreet and customers are not expected to stare. Bringing in one's own drugs is perfectly acceptable, but only the most reckless would attempt to establish a dealership on these premises, which come under the jurisdiction of a licensing system with priorities close to the management's heart. There are seldom any casualties. The people who cannot perform are out on the street, and the enterprise of dreams as enacted by staff and punters alike is well rehearsed to the point of automation. The club thrives on self-control, and it would be criminal to exhibit any loosening of inhibitions. Dealers, staff, and customers operate a protocol of control that enables money and élite leisure to coexist. This is an ideal of late twentieth-century recreation that creates a demand that can only be met by serious criminality. But at the lower end there is serious money to be made from exploiting a demand that, while related to the Armani army of the night, bears a close resemblance to various eras of youth culture and their interrelated markets.[110]

NEW FACES

Straddling both the economic and hedonistic strands of contemporary serious criminality are those emergent practitioners for whom market viability and hedonistic and/or addictive consumption merge. The drugs trade does not constitute a homogeneous economic activity and from the unlikely ranks of user-dealers can emerge some of the more committed, skilled, and organized practitioners. As Dunlap *et al.* vividly and persuasively argue,[111] for user-dealers consistency and longevity within the market-place proffers more than mere economic viability, and the fragmented nature of trading environments and their consequent cultures, the lack of enabling 'underworlds', has spawned criminal forms that owe more to the everyday tribulations inherent in any small business than to the semi-mythical contingencies of traditional professional crime. Yet the criminal status of these non-traditional practitioners cannot be dismissed, for their lack of affiliation to these traditional networks creates cognitive problems that must be resolved along with the everyday accounting conundrums created by corner-shop economics.

In the world of illegal drug sales, the opposition of government and the absence of formal training means that individuals must discover by themselves how to deal with the complex contingencies involved in selling drugs. . . . They must learn how to obtain supplies of high quality drugs to sell; create retail sales units; recruit buyers; avoid arrest, incarceration, and violence from competitors or customers; and handle and account for large amounts of cash, while evading both formal and informal sanctions. . . . Perhaps their most difficult challenge however is to limit their own drug consumption so that they sell to 're-up', or purchase more wholesale units of drugs.[112]

Indeed it is such operatives who are best equipped to manipulate highly localized markets, for it is they that engage, albeit tangentially, with every level of the market having links (several stages removed) with importers, yet maintaining crucial links with users and street dealers. Their apparently complex motives for market engagement should not be allowed to shroud their crucial function as criminal operatives functioning at the fulcrum of contemporary criminal entrepreneurship. The internal cultural perception of the adverse effects on business of criminal entrepreneurs using certain drugs can, as in the case of Wayne,[113] lead to those individuals being isolated from mainstream activity and forced into a very specific subculture that is built around an especially debilitating commodity and highly volatile market. As Davis notes, 'It is important to remember that crack is not simply cheap cocaine . . . but a far more lethal form. Whether or not it is actually the most addictive substance known to science, as originally claimed, it remains an absolute commodity enslaving its consumers.'[114]

For despite the depiction of economic competence that is vividly portrayed by Dunlap *et al.*, the switch from cocaine to crack, or, as Davis has it, 'from haute cuisine to fast food',[115] provokes a stance amongst even the most hedonistic serious criminals[116] that would appear to support the view of Williams that 'Most dealers see crack smokers as obsessive consumers who cannot take care of business . . . Snorters however, can use the drug and still take care of business.'[117]

As was clearly indicated in Chapters 2 and 3, traditional strategies and inherited resources remain, albeit mediated by the realities of the contemporary marketplace, highly regarded even amongst those groups which appear to be engaging with segments of the illegal market-place that are often regarded as being far removed from core traditional concerns.[118]

However, although it is difficult to analyse precisely, traditional limitations imposed by gender expectations would appear to be breaking down. As Moira's story suggests,[119] there are now opportunities for women within serious crime via the drug trade that were unthinkable within markets less inclined towards the orthodoxies of trade and the nurturing of entrepreneurship. Moira's strategy of exploiting sexist expectations also indicates a realistic and highly pragmatic recognition of the limitations and advantages of her gender, particularly in relation to the ever-present threat of violence. Both Dunlap *et al.*[120] and, more forcibly, Fagan,[121] in their studies of drug careers and their enabling economies, claim that, in a development that finds parallel in the legitimate economy, where labour, like the mode of production within which it is framed, has become fragmented as long-established forms of production have become redundant,[122] we can increasingly expect women to become involved in serious criminality. As Durk and Silverman noted, the drug business, for all its faults, is an equal opportunity employer.[123] Fagan has located female involvement in the drug economy as indicative of crucial alterations to the social controls that had prevailed in poor urban neighbourhoods, changes to the structural circumstances of women living in these neighbourhoods, and most importantly a decline in the social status of young men: 'The declining status of young men may have diminished their "gatekeeper" and mediating roles in both conventional and street networks in poor neighbourhoods.'[124]

The very specific contingencies of cocaine markets were seen as relatively open to women, who are able to achieve a measure of status that has traditionally been denied to them within street networks. Together the contributions of Dunlap et al. and Fagen do suggest that the heavily gendered world of professional criminals may be showing signs of altering in accord with the socioeconomic environments that hosts it.

WHACKING PEOPLE

Within serious-crime groups violence replaces the bureaucracy of normative capitalist market economics. It is 'Discharged precisely, unambiguously, continuously, and with as much speed as possible'.[125]

Bureaucratic regimes rationally structure and regulate legitimate markets, and criminal entrepreneurs use violence in a similar fashion. Markets can be established and regulated via the use of violence, market roles established, and hierarchies confirmed. However, the extent of this violence, as McVicar has observed, 'goes far beyond the use of force in the committal of money-making crimes'.[126] Indeed violence of an apparently irrational kind is common, for both serious-crime groups and their personnel maintain their identities through engagement with any form of violent action, whether or not it is orientated towards rational market objectives. In this respect professional criminals can, by using apparently irrational violence, engender a sense of fear that in turn enables an ordered environment within which violence is a rarity. As Block has noted, 'Feuds and vendettas are endemic'[127] within the serious-crime community, and to impose a template of economic rationality upon all their violent activities is somehow to separate personal and occupational identities in a way that distortedly neatens the mayhem that is integral to the social realities of most of the professional criminals featured in this book.

Most of them live in a 'shifting, changing, bickering, competitive, murderous social world',[128] and within such an environment violence becomes a 'cultural expectation'.[129] Indeed it 'runs like a bright thread through the fabric of life',[130] and Danny, Chris, Jimmy, and the characters in Chapter 6 are obliged to engage in combat, for their location within the market-place is heavily reliant upon their reputations as fighters. This use of a traditional masculine strategy within the arena of the contemporary market indicates that there is a powerful sense of continuity within their inherited identities. As Daly and Wilson have indicated, 'a man's reputation depends in part upon the maintenance of a credible threat of violence'.[131]

The disruption of the iconography of working-class labour identity, and in particular the passing of images of muscular, yet essentially altruistic, artisans, have left us with few contemporary images that have any resonance with past eras; the fighter is one. The fighting man as money-maker is another. These individuals stand out even amongst their peers for their total commitment to violent action, a commitment that, as Jimmy's career clearly indicates,[132] is not bounded by legal or cultural convention or restrained by commercial instrumentality. Commercial instrumentality can, however, manifest itself as a by-product of extreme violence. There is money to be made, but the business must never detract from the personal.

When they 'do business', they are also doing violence. A deal is always to their benefit and the punter's detriment. There are no codes, no rules, no resort to the courts, and ombudsmen rarely sport tattoos. Economic rationality and personal pleasure are constantly renegotiated concepts that must be comprehended through shifting identities and increasingly fragmented cultural foundations.[133]

As traditional male employment has, in its working-class manifestation, all but disappeared, the cultural authority of men can be re-established by emphasizing those elements of their cultural inheritance that remain crucial to continuity.[134] Violence is one such way of holding on to cultural authority, and, as Bauman indicates, 'Cultural authorities turn themselves into market forces, become commodities, compete with other commodities, legitimise their value through the selling capacity they attain.'[135]

The ability of Danny and Chris,[136] Jimmy,[137] and Gary[138] to transcend the rationality that normally informs the violence of criminal entrepreneurs is both a market resource and a restraint on trade. It functions as a double-edged sword of wealth and grief which, if wielded indiscriminately, creates a maelstrom that negates the notion that serious criminality is an entirely rational commercial activity that can be comprehended as a mirror, or perverse facsimile, of legitimate business. Violence affords criminals the cultural collateral upon which their entrepreneurial activities are based. Violence also enables them to sustain a semblance of neighbourhood and self-respect at times of economic slump. As is apparent from an analysis of the careers of Chris, Danny, Jimmy, and Gary, hard men in hard times can find their violence a profound handicap to good business. But consistency is everything to men of violence, and they are obliged to respond to a perceived slight to self or to family with the same level of ferocity and commitment as they would to a threat to their commercial viability.

As Katz has indicated, hard men are always vulnerable, for as they 'persevere without limitation until they dominate, then they force others to confront the same choice'.[139] Such confrontations can take place within public, private, familial, or commercial domains, and may produce outcomes which are financially beneficial or calamitous. Either way they are committed to total physical domination, and the more irrational the level of violence, the greater the transcendence of rationality and the higher their stock.

In addition, while non-instrumental violence lends the actor the status of mad dog, nutter, or psycho,[140] it also manufactures a disordered space that can inspire innovation. For instance, both Ronnie Kray's killing of George Cornell and his brother Reggie's killing of Jack McVitie were apparently non-instrumental slaughters inspired by the desire to avenge personal insults.[141] Yet the killings reinforced the mythic reputations of the twins and enhanced their market value, albeit briefly, by transcending the parameters of hard man narratives to the extent that any opposition would result in fatality. However, the killings served to create a new order by making police action inevitable[142] and paving the way for more flexible low-profile serious-crime groups that were ideally suited to the entrepreneurial criminal opportunity structures of the late twentieth century. As Douglas has remarked, 'Granted that disorder spoils pattern, it also provides the materials of pattern. Order implies restriction; from all possible materials, a limited selection has been made and from all possible relations a limited set has been used. So disorder by implication is unlimited. . . . it is destructive to existing patterns . . . It symbolises both danger and power.'[143]

The cultural settings within which this disorder is negotiated provide a cognitive frame for the recognition of the coherence and materially based relevance of any emergent new order. Consequently, the vanguard of the new order will also be the caretakers of the old, teasing out those essences of past performance that might contribute to competent future performance. The family firms that replaced the Krays embraced the essences of entrepreneurial violence with a pathological edge that the Krays had inherited from the gangsters and cobblestone fighters of the 1930s and 1940s.[144] Whether the action is aimed at money, honour, or hedonism, there are no half measures. As world heavyweight champion Mike Tyson explained in the build-up to a title defence, 'If I don't kill him it don't count.'

Violence becomes an obligation that is accumulated in social networks, and

this obligation can be a creative or destructive force, creating identities and re-
inforcing networks or destroying temporary working arrangements. Networks of
professional crime have an unerring habit of emerging on the same fertile ground.
This cultural slash-and-burn technique ensures that the next generation grows
stronger and quicker, and, initially at least, devoid of root-weakening off-shoots.

PAIN AND MONEY

This book has been about those citizens amongst us who for fun and money are
committed to robbing, hurting, and dealing in illegal commodities. Along the
way they develop powerful histories based in sacred places inhabited by icons
of competence. They engage in practices that are often inseparable from those
of conventional business, and some become addicted to drink or drugs while
others are irresistibly drawn to violence regardless of pecuniary consideration.

A neat conclusion to this book would be out of character with a study that has
sought to deny the authenticity of conventional criminal narratives. There will
always be complementary or alternative narratives from the police or from the
next generation of professional criminals. Debates concerning methodology, both
sociological and criminal, will inevitably be ongoing. The recidivist academics
and journalists who make a living from crime will age, learn the error of their
ways and retire, and the old lags go out of print. But someone out there will be
'at it', making drugs in their bathrooms, seeking a monopoly in the new black
markets of body parts, or some variation on pornography, stealing, forging,
buying, selling. Pain and money will never go out of fashion, and the ability to
impose the former in exchange for the latter always looks good on one's CV.

All economic systems have the inherent potential to mutate at times of crisis,
and the very status of serious crime ensures a constant state of flux that makes
it difficult to pin down and analyse, let alone wage war against. Yet professional
crime and the activities that it promotes are so common, their methods so familiar, and their basic precepts so inherent to our society that analysis is relatively
simple when compared to the prospect of eliminating it from the fabric in which
our culture is bound.

Notes

Notes to Introduction

1 J. Ball *et al.*, *Cops and Robbers* (London, 1978).
2 See J. Pearson, *The Profession of Violence* (London, 1973) for an overview.
3 D. Hobbs, 'Peers, Careers and Academic Fears', in D. Hobbs and T. May (eds.), *Interpreting the Field* (Oxford, 1993).
4 M. Levi, 'Violent Crime', in M. Maguire *et al.* (eds.), *The Oxford Handbook of Criminology* (Oxford, 1994), 345.
5 See the excellent T. Williams *et al.*, 'Personal Safety in Dangerous Places', *Journal of Contemporary Ethnography*, 21 (1992), 343–7.
6 J. Katz, *Seductions of Crime* (New York, 1988), p. vii.
7 Hobbs, 'Peers, Careers and Academic Fears'.
8 R. Wright and S. Decker, *Burglars on the Job* (Boston, 1994), 213.
9 N. Polsky, *Hustlers, Beats and Others* (Harmondsworth, 1971), 118.
10 Ibid. 120–1.
11 E. Sutherland and D. Cressey, *The Principles of Criminology* (Philadelphia, 1970), 68.
12 I. Solway and J. Waters, 'Working the Corner', in R. S. Weppner (ed.), *Street Ethnography* (Beverly Hills, Calif., 1977).
13 See Wright and Decker, *Burglars on the Job*, 210–13.
14 W. Chambliss, 'On the Paucity of Research on Organised Crime', *American Sociologist*, 10 (1975), 39.
15 Cf. M. Bulmer, *The Chicago School of Sociology* (Chicago, 1984), 97.
16 M. S. Fleisher, *Burnout in Violent Criminal Careers*, Paper presented at 1993 American Society of Criminology, Phoenix, Arizona, 3.
17 *Burglars on the Job*.
18 See Cohen's intro. and comm. in W. Probyn, *Angel Face* (London, 1977) and K. Plummer, *Documents of Life* (London, 1983).
19 The best British examples are B. Hill, *Boss of Britain's Underworld* (London, 1955), H. Ward, *Buller* (London, 1974), Probyn, *Angel Face*, J. McVicar, *McVicar by Himself* (London, 1979), R. Kray and R. Kray, *Our Story* (London, 1989), R. Kray, *Born Fighter* (London, 1991), C. Richardson, *My Manor* (London, 1992), T. Lambrianou, *Inside the Firm* (London, 1992), F. Fraser, *Mad Frank* (London, 1994), and E. Mason, *Inside Story* (London, 1994).
20 See e.g. G. Tremmlet, *Little Legs* (London, 1989).
21 D. Downes and P. Rock, *Understanding Deviance* (Oxford, 1982), ch. 3.
22 J. Platt, 'The Chicago School and Firsthand Data', *History of the Human Sciences*, 7/1 (Feb. 1994), 57.
23 Bulmer, *The Chicago School of Sociology*.
24 Platt, 'The Chicago School and Firsthand Data'.
25 W. I. Thomas and F. Znaniecki, *The Polish Peasant in Europe and America* (New York, 1927).
26 E. Sutherland, *The Professional Thief* (Chicago, 1937).
27 A. B. N. Hollingshead, 'Behaviour Systems as a Field for Research', *American Journal of Sociology*, 4 (1939), 816–22.
28 See also J. Landesco, *Organised Crime in Chicago* (Chicago, 1968).
29 Notably that of D. W. Maurer, *The Whizz Mob* (New Haven, 1955).
30 E. Lemert, 'The Behaviour of the Systematic Check Forger', *Social Problems*, 6 (1958), 141–9.
31 President's Commission on Law Enforcement and Administration of Justice, *Task Force Report* (Washington, 1967), ch. 3.
32 P. Letkemann, *Crime as Work* (Englewood Cliffs, NJ, 1973).
33 A. Block, *Masters of Paradise* (New Brunswick, 1991).

34 W. J. Einstadter, 'The Social Organisation of Armed Robbery', *Social Problems*, 17 (1969), 64–83.

35 J. A. Mack and H. J. Kerner, *The Crime Industry* (Lexington, Mass., 1975).

36 Ibid. 178.

37 See M. E. Walsh, *The Fence* (Westport, Conn., 1977), M. Walsh and D. Chappell, 'Operational Parameters in the Stolen Property System', *Journal of Criminal Justice*, 2 (1974), 113–29, D. J. Steffensmeier, *The Fence* (Totowa, NJ, 1986), C. Klockars, *The Professional Fence* (London, 1975), M. Maguire and T. Bennett, *Burglary in a Dwelling* (London, 1982), ch. 4, and Wright and Decker, *Burglars on the Job*, ch. 6.

38 N. Shover, 'The Social Organisation of Burglary', *Social Problems*, 20 (1973), 499–514.

39 H. R. Holzman, 'The Serious Habitual Property Offender as Moonlighter', *Journal of Criminal Law and Criminology*, 73 (1983), 1774–92, and N. Polsky, 'The Hustler', *Social Problems*, 12 (1964), 3–15.

40 See e.g. Maurer, *The Whizz Mob*.

41 Shover, 'The Social Organisation of Burglary', 512.

42 Sutherland, *The Professional Thief*, 197.

43 J. Irwin, *The Felon* (Englewood Cliffs, NJ, 1970) and J. Irwin and D. Cressey, 'Thieves, Convicts and the Inmate Culture', *Social Problems*, 10 (1962), 142–55.

44 Irwin, *The Felon*, 8.

45 Irwin and Cressey, 'Thieves, Convicts and the Inmate Culture'; see also S. Cohen and L. Taylor, *Psychological Survival* (Harmondsworth, 1972), ch. 7, J. McVicar, 'Violence in Prisons', in P. Marsh and A. Campbell (eds.), *Aggression and Violence* (Oxford, 1982), Mason, *Inside Story*.

46 L. Taylor, *In the Underworld* (Oxford, 1984), 76.

47 President's Commission, *Task Force Report*, 98.

48 Ball *et al.*, *Cops and Robbers*, Jennings *et al.*, *Scotland Yard's Cocaine Connection* (London, 1991), M. Short, *Lundy* (London, 1992).

49 J. A. Inciardi, 'The Pickpocket and his Victim', *Victimology*, 1 (1976), 141–9.

50 M. McIntosh, 'Changes in the Organisation of Thieving', in S. Cohen (ed.), *Images of Deviance* (Harmondsworth, 1971).

51 Shover, 'The Social Organisation of Burglary'.

52 Letkemann, *Crime as Work*.

53 D. Luckenbill, 'Generating Compliance', *Urban Life*, 10 (Apr. 1981), 25–46.

54 See E. Goffman, 'On Cooling the Mark Out', *Psychiatry*, 15 (1952), 451–63, for an in-depth exploration of the maintenance of compliance; see also E. Schur, 'A Sociological Analysis of Confidence Swindling', *Journal of Criminal Law, Criminology and Police Science*, 48 (1957), 296–304.

55 K. Levi, 'Becoming a Hit Man', *Urban Life*, 10 (Apr. 1981), 47–63.

56 J. Mack, 'Full-Time Miscreants, Delinquent Neighbourhoods and Criminal Networks', *British Journal of Sociology*, 15 (1964), 38–53.

57 A. Block, *The Business of Crime* (Boulder, Colo., 1991).

58 F. Pearce, *Crimes of the Powerful* (London, 1976).

59 D. Hobbs, *Doing the Business* (Oxford, 1988).

60 N. Dorn *et al.*, *Traffickers* (London, 1992), 31–62.

61 J. E. Wideman, *Brothers and Keepers* (New York, 1985), J. S. Gibbs and P. L. Shelley, 'Life in the Fast Lane', *Journal of Research in Crime and Delinquency*, 19 (1982), 299–330, R. Pruis and S. Irini, *Hookers, Rounders and Desk Clerks* (Toronto, 1980).

62 Block, *Masters of Paradise* and *The Business of Crime*, and M. Levi, *Regulating Fraud* (London, 1987).

63 W. J. Chambliss, *On the Take* (Bloomington, Ind., 1978).

64 Levi, *Regulating Fraud*, 194.

65 Ibid. 3.

66 M. McIntosh, *The Organisation of Crime* (London, 1975).

67 J. Langer, 'Drug Entrepreneurs and Dealing Culture', *Social Problems*, 24 (1977), 377–86, N. Dorn and N. South, 'Drug Markets and Enforcement', *British Journal of Criminology*, 30/2 (1990), 171–88, and T. Williams, *The Cocaine Kids* (Reading, Mass., 1989).

68 V. Ruggeiro, 'Brixton, London', *International Journal of Drug Policy*, 4/2 (1993), 83–90, and P. Adler and P. Adler, 'Shifts and Oscillations in Deviant Careers', *Social Problems*, 31 (1983), 195–207.

69 D. Hobbs and C. Dunagen, *Serious Crime Networks* (Durham, forthcoming).
70 Ruggeiro, 'Brixton, London'.
71 Hobbs and Dunnighan, *Serious Crime Networks*.
72 Adler and Adler, 'Shifts and Oscillations in Deviant Careers'.
73 A. Block, *East Side–West Side* (Newark, NJ, 1983).
74 Katz, *Seductions of Crime* (New York, 1988).
75 D. Walsh, *Heavy Business* (London, 1986), ch. 3.
76 Walsh, *Heavy Business*, 57.
77 Taylor, *In the Underworld*, McVicar, *McVicar by Himself*, Ball *et al.*, *Cops and Robbers*.
78 Cf. R. Burrows (ed.), *Deciphering the Enterprise Culture* (London, 1991), P. Heelas and P. Morris (eds.), *The Values of the Enterprise Culture* (London, 1992).
79 N. Shover, *Ageing Criminals* (Beverly Hills, Calif., 1985).
80 Mason, *Inside Story*, 274–5.
81 J. J. Tobias, 'The Crime Industry', *British Journal of Criminology*, 2 (1968), 247–58.
82 See I. Taylor, 'The Concept of Social Cost in Free Market Theory and the Social Costs of Free Market Policies', in I. Taylor (ed.), *The Social Effect of Free Market Policies* (Hemel Hempstead, 1991).
83 D. Hobbs, 'Professional and Organised Crime', in Maguire *et al.* (eds.), *The Oxford Handbook of Criminology*.
84 Block, *East Side–West Side*, 249.
85 Mack, 'Full-Time Miscreants, Delinquent Neighbourhoods and Criminal Networks'.
86 Cf. R. Warshow, *The Gangster as Tragic Hero* (Partisan Review, 1948), D. Hebdige, 'The Kray Twins', Occasional Paper no. 21, Centre for Contemporary Cultural Studies, Birmingham University, 1974, 10, D. Hebdige, 'Sub-cultural Conflict and Criminal Performance in Fulham', Occasional Paper no. 25, Centre for Contemporary Cultural Studies, Birmingham University, 1977, 56–8.
87 D. Cressey, *Criminal Organisation* (London, 1972), 45.

Notes to Chapter 2

1 D. Hobbs and D. Robins, 'The Boy Done Good', *Sociological Review*, 39/3 (1991), 571.
2 See Chapter 5.

Notes to Chapter 3

1 The attractions of this business are vividly described by Arthur Harding: 'you can't submit to discipline, you have to be your own master. So, you pick something where you have to depend on your wits. It's a precarious sort of a living, but you are not under a foreman' (R. Samuel, *East End Underworld* (London, 1981)).
2 This point is elaborated on by T. Lambrianou: 'And if you didn't have a family of brothers with you, you were nothing. Brothers were your strength . . . all the major villains of our generation were brothers' (*Inside the Firm* (London, 1992), 22).
3 For confirmation of the lack of planning involved in most armed robberies, see J. Katz, *Seductions of Crime* (New York, 1988).
4 But it was suggested to me both by members of Jimmy's family and by ex-colleagues of his that on at least three occasions people had been injured as a result of Jimmy letting loose with a shotgun. It was also reported that the injuries sustained by one security guard were serious. This tendency by armed robbers to understate the amount and level of violence they used is documented in D. Campbell, *That was Business, This is Personal* (London, 1991), ch. 1. This denial is a means by which the robber can maintain the moral dominance that he had originally developed in order to commit the crime (see Katz, *Seductions of Crime*, 169–76). As the retired armed robber indicates in Ch. 1, physical superiority and brute force are not sufficient: a rather more subtle set of competencies are required. The denial of violent activity serves, therefore, to

enhance rather than contradict the reputations of those for whom savagery constitutes master status in addition to providing a marketable resource.

Note to Chapter 4

1 See Ch. 1.

Notes to Chapter 6

1 The Thatcher government's focus upon football hooliganism and the plethora of police operations that followed are dealt with by G. Armstrong and D. Hobbs, 'Tackled from Behind', in R. Giulianotti *et al.* (eds.), *Football Violence and Social Identity* (London, 1994).
2 For an excellent synopsis of 'post-Ibiza' youth culture which includes reference to the entrepreneurial exploitation of some of its key elements, see H. Rietveld, 'Living the Dream', in S. Redhead (ed.), *Rave Off* (Aldershot, 1993).

Note to Chapter 7

1 See Appendix.

Notes to Chapter 8

1 See D. Matza and G. Sykes, 'Delinquency and Subterranean Values', *American Sociological Review*, 26/5 (1961).
2 E. Sutherland, *The Professional Thief* (Chicago, 1937).
3 I. J. Cohen, *Structuration Theory* (London, 1989), 156.
4 A. Block, *East Side–West Side* (Newark, NJ, 1983).
5 Z. Bauman, *Intimations of Postmodernity* (London, 1992), 52.
6 Ibid., Z. Bauman, *Legislators and Interpreters* (Cambridge, 1989), and D. Hobbs, *Doing the Business* (Oxford, 1988).
7 Z. Bauman, *Freedom* (Milton Keynes, 1988), 66–7.
8 Bauman, *Intimations of Postmodernity*, 98.
9 Ibid.
10 D. Morgan, *Discovering Men* (London, 1992), 45.
11 Hobbs, *Doing the Business*.
12 M. Davis, *City of Quartz* (London, 1990), 304–6.
13 P. Cohen, *Subcultural Conflict and Working Class Community*, Working Papers in Cultural Studies no. 2 (Birmingham, 1972).
14 See Davis, *City of Quartz*, ch. 5.
15 Hobbs, *Doing the Business*.
16 A. Giddens, *Modernity and Self-Identity* (Cambridge, 1991), 17.
17 A. Giddens, *A Contemporary Critique of Historical Materialism* (London, 1981), 63.
18 Giddens, *Modernity and Self-Identity*, 19.
19 D. Hobbs, 'Business as a Master Metaphor', in R. Burrows (ed.), *Deciphering the Enterprise Culture* (London, 1991).
20 D. Hobbs, 'Professional and Organised Crime', in M. Maguire *et al.* (eds.), *The Oxford Handbook of Criminology* (Oxford, 1994), 447.

21 See C. Richardson, *My Manor* (London, 1992), ch. 10, and T. Lambrianou, *Inside the Firm* (London, 1992), 238–41.
22 C. Richardson, *My Manor* (London, 1992), and R. Kray, *Born Fighter* (London, 1991), 137–8.
23 F. Fraser, *Mad Frank* (London, 1994), 147.
24 E. Mason, *Inside Story* (London, 1994), 186.
25 Fraser, *Mad Frank*, 147.
26 Lambrianou, *Inside the Firm*, 102–3.
27 See A. Blok, *The Mafia of a Sicilian Village* (New York, 1974), 171–6.
28 Giddens, *Modernity and Self-Identity*, 3.
29 A. M. Rose, *Human Behaviour and Social Processes* (London, 1962), 14.
30 See Ch. 1.
31 B. Anderson, *Imagined Communities* (London, 1983).
32 Z. Bauman, *Intimations of Postmodernity* (London, 1992).
33 Ibid.
34 R. Lacey, *Little Man* (New York, 1991), 394.
35 D. Chaney, *The Cultural Turn* (London, 1994), 140–4.
36 Z. Bauman, *Modernity and Ambivalence* (Cambridge, 1993), 1–17.
37 See the descriptions of the murder of Jack McVitie in Lambrianou, *Inside the Firm*, 7–17, R. Kray and R. Kray, *Our Story* (London, 1989), 85–94, C. Kray and J. Sykes, *Me and my Brothers* (London, 1977), 197–202, and J. Pearson, *The Profession of Violence* (London, 1973), 212–21.
38 See R. Knight, *Black Knight* (London, 1990), 213–14.
39 R. Murphy, *Smash and Grab* (London, 1993), and J. Morton, *Gangland* (London, 1993).
40 W. Benjamin, *Illuminations* (London, 1973), 265.
41 Kray and Kray, 225.
42 D. Bell, *The End of Ideology* (London, 1961), 140–1.
43 Burrows (ed.), *Deciphering the Enterprise Culture*.
44 J. Albanese, *Organised Crime in America* (Cincinnati, 1989), 101.
45 Giddens, *Modernity and Self-Identity*, 1.
46 D. Chaney, *The Cultural Turn* (London, 1994).
47 Chaney, *The Cultural Turn*, 149.
48 Giddens, *Modernity and Self-Identity*, 1.
49 A. Block, 'Contemporary Waste Issues', *Environmental Liability Law Review* (1992); repr. in *Space, Time and Organised Crime* (New Brunswick, 1994), and A. Block and F. Scarpitti, *Poisoning for Profit* (New York, 1985).
50 A. D. King, Introduction, in A. D. King (ed.), *Culture Globalisation and the World System* (London, 1991), 6.
51 A. Giddens, *The Consequences of Modernity* (Cambridge, 1990), 64, and Giddens, *Modernity and Self-Identity*, 22.
52 A. Block, *Masters of Paradise* (New Brunswick, 1991) and *The Business of Crime* (Boulder, Colo., 1991), 1–26.
53 J. Roebuck and G. Windham, 'Professional Theft', in G. Waldo (ed.), *Criminal Careers* (Beverly Hills, 1983), G. Salgado, *The Elizabethan Underworld* (London, 1977), and G. Howson, *Thief Taker General* (New York, 1971).
54 P. B. Munsche, *Gentlemen and Poachers* (Cambridge, 1981), D. Hay, 'Property, Authority and the Criminal Law', in D. Hay *et al.*, *Albion's Fatal Tree* (London, 1975), J. A. Sharpe, *Crime in Early Modern England 1550–1750* (London, 1984).
55 D. A. Low, *Thieves' Kitchen* (London, 1982).
56 G. Stedman-Jones, *Outcast London* (Oxford, 1971); see also R. Samuel, *East End Underworld* (London, 1981).
57 P. Rawlings, *Drunks, Whores and Idle Apprentices* (London, 1992).
58 D. Downes and P. Rock, *Understanding Deviance* (Oxford, 1982), 58.
59 H. Mayhew, *London's Underworld*, (ed.), P. Quennell (London, 1950).
60 P. Rock, *Deviant Behaviour* (London, 1973), 30.
61 B. Werlen, *Society, Action and Space* (London, 1993), 3, cited in Chaney, *The Cultural Turn*, 148.

62 R. Shields, *Places on the Margin* (London, 1990).

63 Hobbs, *Doing the Business*.

64 W. Miller, 'Lower Class Culture as a Generating Milieu of Gang Delinquency', *Journal of Social Issues*, 14 (1958), 7.

65 A. Feldman, *Formations of Violence* (Chicago, 1991), 53.

66 D. Campbell, *That was Business, This is Personal* (London, 1991), and N. Dorn et al., *Traffickers* (London, 1992).

67 Block, *The Business of Crime*, 15.

68 S. Lash and J. Urry, *The End of Organised Capitalism* (Cambridge, 1987).

69 F. Hirsch, *Social Limits to Growth* (New York, 1978).

70 J. Curran and R. Blackburn, 'Changes in the Context of Enterprise', in *Paths of Enterprise* (London, 1991), 184.

71 Dorn et al., *Traffickers*, 3–59; see M. Piore and C. Sabel, *The Second Industrial Divide* (New York, 1984).

72 See Ch. 5.

73 Giddens, *Modernity and Self-Identity*, 21–2.

74 A. Giddens, *Central Problems in Social Theory* (London, 1979), 65–6.

75 W. J. Chambliss, *On the Take* (Bloomington, Ind., 1987), 8.

76 President's Commission on Law Enforcement and Administration of Justice, *Task Force Report* (Washington, 1967), P. Letkemann, *Crime as Work* (Englewood Cliffs, NJ, 1973), H. R. Holzman, 'The Serious Habitual Property Offender as Moonlighter', *Journal of Criminal Law and Criminology*, 73 (1983), 1774–92, N. Polsky, 'The Hustler', *Social Problems*, 12 (1964), 3–15, N. Polsky, *Hustlers, Beats and Others* (Harmondsworth, 1971), and N. Shover, 'The Social Organisation of Burglary', *Social Problems*, 20 (1973), 499–514.

77 I. J. Cohen, *Structuration Theory* (London, 1989), 62.

78 S. Nadel, *The Theory of Social Structure* (London, 1957).

79 Block, 'Contemporary Waste Issues', 13; cf. D. R. Cressey, *Theft of the Nation* (New York, 1969).

80 R. Aniskiewicz, 'Metatheoretical Issues in the Study of Organised Crime', Paper presented at the Annual Meeting of the American Society of Criminology, Phoenix, Arizona, 27–30 Oct., 1.

81 M. Haller, 'Illegal Enterprise', *Criminology*, 28/2 (1990), 207–35; see Chs. 4 and 6.

82 See Chs. 2 and 3.

83 J. Habermas, *The Theory of Communicative Action*, i (London, 1984).

84 N. Pileggi, *Wise Guy* (London, 1987), 39.

85 N. Shover and D. Honaker, 'The Socially Bounded Decision Making of Persistent Property Offenders', *Howard Journal*, 31 (Nov. 1991), 276–93.

86 J. Katz, *Seductions of Crime* (New York, 1988), 215.

87 See Ch. 5.

88 Katz, *Seductions of Crime*, 236.

89 See Ch. 7.

90 L. Taylor, 'Ducking and Diving', *New Society* (6 Jan. 1983), 14.

91 Katz, *Seductions of Crime*, 230.

92 T. Bennett and R. Wright, *Burglars or Burglary* (Aldershot, 1984), F. Feeney, 'Robbers as Decision Makers', in D. B. Cornish and R. V. Clarke (eds.), *The Reasoning Criminal* (New York, 1986), D. Walsh, *Heavy Business* (London, 1986).

93 Shover and Honaker, 'The Socially Bounded Decision Making of Persistent Property Offenders', 282.

94 Ibid. 283.

95 L. Taylor, *In the Underworld* (Oxford, 1984), 169.

96 J. E. Wideman, *Brothers and Keepers* (New York, 1985), 131.

97 Ch. 1.

98 Ch. 7.

99 Ch. 1.

100 C. Rojek, *Ways of Escape* (London, 1993), 97–135.

101 H. Lefebvre, *The Survival of Capitalism* (London, 1976), 84.

102 R. J. Anderson et al., *Working for Profit* (Aldershot, 1989).

103 Chs. 4 and 5.
104 Chs. 6 and 7.
105 Z. Bauman, *Modernity and Ambivalence* (Cambridge, 1993), 13.
106 Ch. 7.
107 Taylor, *In the Underworld*, 93; see Jason, Ch. 7.
108 See Jock, Ch. 7.
109 Ch. 7.
110 Ch. 6.
111 E. Dunlap *et al.*, 'A Successful Female Crack Dealer', *Deviant Behaviour*, 15 (1994), 1–25.
112 Ibid. 4–5.
113 Ch. 7.
114 Davis, *City of Quartz*, 314.
115 Ibid. 311.
116 See Ch. 7.
117 T. Williams, *The Cocaine Kids* (Reading, Mass., 1989).
118 Fraser, *Mad Frank*, 228–9.
119 Ch. 1.
120 Dunlap *et al.*, 'A Successful Female Crack Dealer'.
121 J. Fagan, 'Women and Drugs Revisited', *Journal of Drug Issues*, 24/2 (1994), 179–225.
122 Lash and Urry, *The End of Organised Capitalism*, and Piore and Sabel, *The Second Industrial Divide*.
123 D. Durk and I. Silverman, *The Pleasant Avenue Connection* (New York: Harper & Row, 1976).
124 Fagan, 'Women and Drugs Revisited', 186.
125 M. Weber, Essays in Sociology (1948), ed. H. Gerth and C. Wright Mills (London, 1991).
126 J. McVicar, 'Blood Sport', *FHM* (May 1994), 66.
127 Block, 'Contemporary Waste Issues', 33.
128 Ibid. 13.
129 M. Wolfgang, *Patterns in Criminal Homicide* (Philadelphia, 1959).
130 G. Sykes, *The Society of Captives* (Princeton, 1958), 102.
131 M. Daly and M. Wilson, *Homicide* (New York, 1988), 128.
132 Ch. 3.
133 Lash and Urry, *The End of Organised Capitalism*.
134 Hobbs, *Doing the Business*, ch. 7.
135 Bauman, *Intimations of Postmodernity*, 452.
136 Ch. 2.
137 Ch. 3.
138 Ch. 6.
139 Katz, *Seductions of Crime*, 100.
140 Ibid. 181–5.
141 Lambrianou, *Inside the Firm*, 7–17, Pearson, *The Profession of Violence*, 201–52, and Kray, *Born Fighter*, 95–7.
142 Hobbs, *Doing the Business*, ch. 3.
143 M. Douglas, *Purity and Danger* (Harmondsworth, 1966), 94.
144 Pearson, *The Profession of Violence*, ch. 1, Kray, *Born Fighter*, Morton, *Gangland*, ch. 1.

Bibliography

ABADINSKY, H., *Organised Crime*, 3rd edn. (Chicago: Nelson Hall, 1991).

ADLER, P., and ADLER, P., 'Shifts and Oscillations in Deviant Careers: The Case of Upper Level Drug Dealers and Smugglers', *Social Problems*, 31 (1983), 195–207.

ALBANESE, J., *Organised Crime in America* (Cincinnati: Anderson, 1989).

ANDERSON, B., *Imagined Communities* (London: Verso, 1983).

ANDERSON, R. J., HUGHES, J. A., and SHARROCK, W. W., *Working for Profit: The Social Organisation of Calculation in an Entrepreneurial Firm* (Aldershot: Avebury, 1989).

ANISKIEWICZ, R., 'Metatheoretical Issues in the Study of Organised Crime', Paper presented at the Annual Meeting of the American Society of Criminology, Phoenix, Arizona, 27–30 Oct. 1993.

ARMSTRONG, G., and HOBBS, D., 'Tackled from Behind', in R. Giulianotti, N. Bonney, and M. Hepworth (eds.), *Football Violence and Social Identity* (London: Routledge, 1994).

BALL, J., *et al.*, *Cops and Robbers* (London: André Deutsch, 1978).

BAUMAN, Z., *Freedom* (Milton Keynes: Open University Press, 1988).

—— *Legislators and Interpreters* (Cambridge: Polity Press, 1989).

—— *Intimations of Postmodernity* (London: Routledge, 1992).

—— *Modernity and Ambivalence* (Cambridge: Polity Press, 1993).

BELL, D., *The End of Ideology* (London: Free Press/Collier-Macmillan, 1961).

BENJAMIN, W., *Illuminations* (London: Fontana, 1973).

BENNETT, T., and Wright, R., *Burglars on Burglary* (Aldershot: Gower, 1984).

BLOCK, A., *East Side–West Side: Organizing Crime in New York 1930–1950* (Newark, NJ: Transaction, 1983).

—— *Masters of Paradise* (New Brunswick: Transaction, 1991).

—— *The Business of Crime* (Boulder, Colo.: Westview Press, 1991).

—— 'The Complex Interests of Attwoods PLC: A Personal Encounter', in F. Pearce and M. Woodiwiss (eds.), *Readings in Crime and Corruption* (London: Macmillan, 1993).

—— 'Contemporary Waste Issues: Environmental Liability Law Review' (1992); repr. in *Space, Time and Organised Crime* (New Brunswick: Transaction, 1994).

—— and SCARPITTI, F., *Poisoning for Profit: The Mafia and Toxic Waste* (New York: William Morrow, 1985).

BLOK, A., *The Mafia of a Sicilian Village* (New York: Harper, 1974).

BULMER, M., *The Chicago School of Sociology* (Chicago: University of Chicago Press, 1984).

BURROWS, R. (ed.), *Deciphering the Enterprise Culture* (London: Routledge, 1991).

CAMPBELL, D., *That was Business, This is Personal* (London: Mandarin, 1991).

CHAMBLISS, W. J., *Box Man* (New York: Harper & Row, 1972).

—— 'On the Paucity of Research on Organised Crime: A Reply to Galliher and Cain', *American Sociologist*, 10 (1975), 36–9.

—— *On the Take* (Bloomington: Indiana University Press, 1978).

CHANEY, D., *The Cultural Turn* (London: Routledge, 1994).

CHESNEY, K., *The Victorian Underworld* (Harmondsworth: Penguin, 1968).

COHEN, I. J., *Structuration Theory: Anthony Giddens and the Constitution of Social Life* (London: Macmillan, 1989).

COHEN, P., *Subcultural Conflict and Working Class Community*, Working Papers in Cultural Studies no. 2 (Birmingham: CCCS, University of Birmingham, 1972).

COHEN, S., and TAYLOR, L., *Psychological Survival* (Harmondsworth: Penguin, 1972).

CRESSEY, D., *Theft of the Nation* (New York: Harper & Row, 1969).

—— *Criminal Organisation* (London: Heinemann, 1972).

CURRAN, J., and BLACKBURN, R., 'Changes in the Context of Enterprise', in *Paths of Enterprise: The Future of Small Business* (London: Routledge, 1991).

DALY, M., and WILSON, M., *Homicide* (New York: de Gruyter, 1988).

DAVIS, M., *City of Quartz* (London: Verso, 1990).

DORN, N., and SOUTH, N., 'Drug Markets and Enforcement', *British Journal of Criminology*, 30/2 (1990), 171–88.

—— MURJI, K., and SOUTH, N., *Traffickers* (London: Routledge, 1992).

DOUGLAS, M., *Purity and Danger* (Harmondsworth: Penguin, 1966).

DOWNES, D., and ROCK, P., *Understanding Deviance* (Oxford: Clarendon Press, 1982).

DUNLAP, E., JOHNSON, B., and MANWAR, A., 'A Successful Female Crack Dealer: Case Study of a Deviant Career', *Deviant Behaviour*, 15 (1994), 1–25.

EINSTADTER, W. J., 'The Social Organisation of Armed Robbery', *Social Problems*, 17 (1969), 64–83.

FAGAN, J., 'Women and Drugs Revisited: Female Participation in the Cocaine Economy', *Journal of Drug Issues*, 24/2 (1994), 179–225.

FEENEY, F., 'Robbers as Decision Makers', in D. B. Cornish and R. V. Clarke (eds.), *The Reasoning Criminal* (New York: Springer-Verlag, 1986).

FELDMAN, A., *Formations of Violence: The Narrative of the Body and Political Terror in Northern Ireland* (Chicago: University of Chicago Press, 1991).

FLEISHER, M. S., *Burnout in Violent Criminal Careers*, Paper presented at Annual Meeting of the American Society of Criminology, Phoenix, Arizona, 1993.

FRASER, F., *Mad Frank* (London: Little Brown, 1994).

GIBBS, J. S., and SHELLEY, P. L., 'Life in the Fast Lane: A Retrospective View by Commercial Thieves', *Journal of Research in Crime and Delinquency*, 19 (1982), 299–330.

GIDDENS, A., *Central Problems in Social Theory* (London: Macmillan, 1979).

—— *A Contemporary Critique of Historical Materialism* (London: Macmillan, 1981).

—— *The Consequences of Modernity* (Cambridge: Polity Press, 1990).

—— *Modernity and Self-Identity* (Cambridge: Polity Press, 1991).

GOFFMAN, E., 'On Cooling the Mark Out: Some Aspects of Adaptation to Failure', *Psychiatry*, 15 (1952), 451–63.

HABERMAS, J., *The Theory of Communicative Action*, i (London: Heinemann, 1984).

HALLER, M., 'Illegal Enterprise: A Theoretical and Historical Interpretation', *Criminology*, 282 (1990), 207–35.

HAY, D., 'Property, Authority and the Criminal Law', in D. Hay, P. Linebaugh, and E. P. Thompson (eds.), *Albion's Fatal Tree* (London: Allen Lane, 1975).

HEBDIGE, D.,'The Kray Twins: A System of Closure', Occasional Paper no. 21, Centre for Contemporary Cultural Studies, Birmingham University, 1974.

—— 'Sub-cultural Conflict and Criminal Performance in Fulham', Occasional Paper no. 25, Centre for Contemporary Cultural Studies, Birmingham University, 1977.

HEELAS, P., and MORRIS, P. (eds.), *The Values of the Enterprise Culture* (London: Routledge, 1992).

HILL, B., *Boss of Britain's Underworld* (London: Naldrett Press, 1955).

HIRSCH, F., *Social Limits to Growth* (New York: Twentieth Century Fund, 1978).

HOBBS, D., *Doing the Business: Entrepreneurship, Detectives and the Working Class in the East End of London* (Oxford: Clarendon Press, 1988).

—— 'Business as a Master Metaphor', in R. Burrows (ed.), *Deciphering the Enterprise Culture* (London: Routledge, 1991).

—— 'Peers, Careers and Academic Fears', in D. Hobbs and T. May (eds.), *Interpreting the Field* (Oxford: Oxford University Press, 1993).

—— 'Professional and Organised Crime', in M. Maguire, M. Morgan, and R. Reiner (eds.), *The Oxford Handbook of Criminology* (Oxford: Oxford University Press, 1994).

—— and DUNNIGHAN, C., *Serious Crime Networks* (Durham: University of Durham, forthcoming).

—— and ROBINS, D., 'The Boy Done Good', *Sociological Review*, 39/3 (1991).

HOHIMER, F., *Violent Streets* (London: Star, 1981).

HOLLINGSHEAD, A. B. N., 'Behaviour Systems as a Field for Research', *American Journal of Sociology*, 4 (1939), 816–22.

HOLZMAN, H. R., 'The Serious Habitual Property Offender as Moonlighter: An Empirical Study of Labour Force Participation among Robbers and Burglars', *Journal of Criminal Law and Criminology*, 73 (1983), 1774–92.

HOWSON, G., *Thief Taker General* (New York: St Martin's Press, 1971).

INCIARDI, J. A., 'The Pickpocket and his Victim', *Victimology*, 1 (1976), 141–9.

IRWIN, J., and CRESSEY, D., 'Thieves, Convicts and the Inmate Culture', *Social Problems*, 10 (1962), 142–55.

—— *The Felon* (Englewood Cliffs, NJ: Prentice-Hall, 1970).

JENNINGS, A., LASHMAR, P., and SIMSON, V., *Scotland Yard's Cocaine Connection* (London: Arrow, 1991).

KATZ, J., *Seductions of Crime* (New York: Basic Books, 1988).

KING, A. D., Introduction, in A. D. King (ed.), *Culture Globalisation and the World System* (London: Macmillan, 1991).

KLOCKARS, C., *The Professional Fence* (London: Tavistock, 1975).

KNIGHT, R., *Black Knight* (London: Century, 1990).

KRAY, C., and SYKES, J., *Me and my Brothers* (London: Everest, 1977).

KRAY, R., *Born Fighter* (London: Arrow, 1991).

—— and KRAY, R., *Our Story* (London: Pan, 1989).

LACEY, R., *Little Man* (New York: Little Brown, 1991).

LAMBRIANOU, T., *Inside the Firm* (London: Pan, 1992).

LANDESCO, J., *Organised Crime in Chicago* (2nd edn. Chicago: University of Chicago Press, 1968).

LANGER, J., 'Drug Entrepreneurs and Dealing Culture', *Social Problems*, 24 (1977), 377–86.

LASH, S., and URRY, J., *The End of Organised Capitalism* (Cambridge: Polity Press, 1987).

LEFEBVRE, H., *The Survival of Capitalism* (London: Allen & Unwin, 1976).

LEMERT, E., 'The Behaviour of the Systematic Check Forger', *Social Problems*, 6 (1958), 141–9.

LETKEMANN, P., *Crime as Work* (Englewood Cliffs, NJ: Prentice-Hall, 1973).

LEVI, K., 'Becoming a Hit Man: Neutralisation in a very Deviant Career', *Urban Life*, 10 (Apr. 1981), 47–63.

LEVI, M., *Regulating Fraud* (London: Tavistock, 1987).

—— 'Developments in Business Crime Control in Europe', in F. Heidensohn and M. Farrell (eds.), *Crime in Europe* (London: Routledge, 1991).

—— 'Violent Crime', in M. Maguire, R. Morgan, and R. Reiner (eds.), *The Oxford Handbook of Criminology* (Oxford: Oxford University Press, 1994).

LOW, D. A., *Thieves' Kitchen: The Regency Underworld* (London: Dent, 1982).

LUCKENBILL, D., 'Generating Compliance: The Case of Robbery', *Urban Life*, 10 (Apr. 1981), 25–46.

MCINTOSH, M., 'Changes in the Organisation of Thieving', in S. Cohen (ed.), *Images of Deviance* (Harmondsworth: Penguin, 1971).

—— *The Organisation of Crime* (London: Macmillan, 1975).

MACK, J., 'Full-Time Miscreants, Delinquent Neighbourhoods and Criminal Networks', *British Journal of Sociology*, 15 (1964), 38–53.

—— and KERNER, H. J., *The Crime Industry* (Lexington, Mass.: Saxon House, Lexington Books, 1975).

MCVICAR, J., *McVicar by Himself* (London: Arrow, 1979).

—— 'Violence in Prisons', in P. Marsh and A. Campbell (eds.), *Aggression and Violence* (Oxford: Blackwell, 1982).

—— 'Blood Sport', *FHM* (May 1994), 64–6.

MAGUIRE, M., and BENNETT, T., *Burglary in a Dwelling* (London: Heinemann, 1982).

MASON, E., *Inside Story* (London: Pan, 1994).

MATZA, D., and SYKES, G., 'Delinquency and Subterranean Values', *American Sociological Review*, 26/5 (1961).

MAURER, D. W., *The Whizz Mob* (New Haven: College and University Press, 1955).

MAYHEW, H., *London Labour and the London Poor*, 4 vols. (1861; fac. edn. London: Dover, 1968).

—— *London's Underworld* (London: Spring Books, 1950).

MILLER, W., 'Lower Class Culture as a Generating Milieu of Gang Delinquency', *Journal of Social Issues*, 14 (1958).

MORGAN, D., *Discovering Men* (London: Routledge, 1992).

MORTON, J., *Gangland: London's Underworld* (London: Warner, 1993).

MUNSCHE, P. B., *Gentlemen and Poachers* (Cambridge: Cambridge University Press, 1981).

MURPHY, R., *Smash and Grab* (London: Faber, 1993).

NADEL, S., *The Theory of Social Structure* (London: Cohen & West, 1957).

Ordinary of Newgates Account: Mary Young. (London: John Applebee, 1741); repr. in P. Rawlings, *Drunks, Whores and Idle Apprentices: Criminal Biographies of the Eighteenth Century* (London: Routledge, 1992).

PEARCE, F., *Crimes of the Powerful* (London: Pluto, 1976).

PEARSON, J., *The Profession of Violence* (London: Granada, 1973).

PILEGGI, N., *Wise Guy* (London: Corgi, 1987).

PIORE, M., and SABEL, C., *The Second Industrial Divide* (New York: Basic Books, 1984).

PLATT, J., 'The Chicago School and Firsthand Data', *History of the Human Sciences*, 7/1 (Feb. 1994), 57–80.

PLUMMER, K., *Documents of Life* (London: Unwin Hyman, 1983).

POLSKY, N., 'The Hustler', *Social Problems*, 12 (1964), 3–15.

—— *Hustlers, Beats and Others* (1967; Harmondsworth: Pelican, 1971).

PRESIDENT'S COMMISSION ON LAW ENFORCEMENT AND ADMINISTRATION OF JUSTICE, *Task Force Report* (Washington: US Goverment Printing Office, 1967), ch. 7.

PROBYN, W., *Angel Face: The Making of a Criminal* (London: Allen & Unwin, 1977).

PRUIS, R., and IRINI, S., *Hookers, Rounders and Desk Clerks: The Social Organisation of a Hotel Community* (Toronto: Gage, 1980).

RAWLINGS, P., *Drunks, Whores and Idle Apprentices* (London: Routledge, 1992).

REUTER, P., *Disorganised Crime* (Cambridge, Mass.: MIT Press, 1984).

—— *Racketeering in Legitimate Industries: A Study in the Economics of Intimidation* (Santa Monica, Calif.: Rand Corporation, 1987).

RICHARDSON, C., *My Manor* (London: Pan, 1992).

RIETVELD, H., 'Living the Dream', in S. Redhead (ed.), *Rave Off: Politics and Deviance in Contemporary Youth Culture* (Aldershot: Avebury, 1993).

ROCK, P., *Deviant Behaviour* (London: Hutchinson, 1973).

ROEBUCK, J., and WINDHAM, G., 'Professional Theft', in G. Waldo (ed.), *Criminal Careers* (Beverly Hills, Calif.: Sage, 1983).

—— —— *Criminal Careers* (Beverly Hills, Calif.: Sage, 1983).

ROJEK, C., *Ways of Escape* (London: Macmillan, 1993).

ROSE, A. M., *Human Behaviour and Social Processes* (London: Routledge & Kegan Paul, 1962).

RUGGEIRO, V., 'Brixton, London: A Drug Culture without a Drug Economy?', *International Journal of Drug Policy*, 4/2 (1993), 83–90.

SALGADO, G., *The Elizabethan Underworld* (London: Dent, 1977).

SAMUEL, R., *East End Underworld: The Life and Times of Arthur Harding* (London: Routledge & Kegan Paul, 1981).

SCHUR, E., 'A Sociological Analysis of Confidence Swindling', *Journal of Criminal Law, Criminology and Police Science*, 48 (1957), 296–304.

SHARPE, J. A., *Crime in Early Modern England 1550–1750* (London: Longman, 1984).

SHIELDS, R., *Places on the Margin: Alternative Geographies of Modernity* (London: Routledge, 1990).

SHORT, M., *Lundy* (London: Grafton, 1992).

SHOVER, N., 'The Social Organisation of Burglary', *Social Problems*, 20 (1973), 499–514.

—— *Ageing Criminals* (Beverly Hills, Calif.: Sage, 1985).

—— and HONAKER, D., 'The Socially Bounded Decision Making of Persistent Property Offenders', *Howard Journal*, 31 (Nov. 1991), 276–93.

SOLWAY, I., and WATERS, J., 'Working the Corner: The Ethics and Legality of Ethnographic Fieldwork among Active Heroin Addicts', in R. S. Weppner (ed.), *Street Ethnography* (Beverly Hills, Calif.: Sage, 1977).

STEDMAN-JONES, G., *Outcast London* (Oxford: Oxford University Press, 1971).

STEFFENSMEIER, D. J., *The Fence: In the Shadow of Two Worlds* (Totowa, NJ: Rowman & Littlefield, 1986).

SUTHERLAND, E., *The Professional Thief* (Chicago: University of Chicago Press, 1937).

—— and CRESSEY, D., *The Principles of Criminology* (8th edn. Philadelphia: Lippincott, 1970).

SYKES, G., *The Society of Captives* (Princeton: Princeton University Press, 1958).

TAYLOR, A., *Women Drug Users: An Ethnography of a Female Injecting Community* (Oxford: Clarendon Press, 1993).

TAYLOR, I., 'The Concept of Social Cost in Free Market Theory and the Social Costs of Free Market Policies', in I. Taylor (ed.), *The Social Effect of Free Market Policies* (Hemel Hempstead: Harvester Wheatsheaf, 1991).

TAYLOR, L., 'Ducking and Diving', *New Society* (6 Jan. 1983), 13–15.

—— *In the Underworld* (Oxford: Blackwell, 1984).

THOMAS, W. I., and ZNANIECKI, F., *The Polish Peasant in Europe and America*, 2 vols. (2nd edn. New York: Knopf, 1927).

TOBIAS, J. J., 'The Crime Industry', *British Journal of Criminology*, 2 (1968), 247–58.

—— *Crime and Police in England 1700–1900* (London: Gill & Macmillan, 1979).

TREMMLET, G., *Little Legs* (London: Unwin Hyman, 1989).

WALSH, D., *Heavy Business* (London: Routledge & Kegan Paul, 1986).

WALSH, M. E., *The Fence* (Westport, Conn.: Greenwood Press, 1977).

—— and CHAPPELL, D., 'Operational Parameters in the Stolen Property System', *Journal of Criminal Justice*, 2 (1974), 113–29.

WARD, H., *Buller* (London: Hodder & Stoughton, 1974).

WARSHOW, R., *The Gangster as Tragic Hero* (Partisan Review, 1948).

WEBER, M., *Essays in Sociology* (1948), ed. H. Gerth and C. Wright Mills (London: Routledge, 1991).

WERLEN, B., *Society, Action and Space* (London: Routledge, 1993).

WIDEMAN, J. E., *Brothers and Keepers* (New York: Penguin, 1985).

WILLIAMS, T., *The Cocaine Kids* (Reading, Mass.: Addison-Wesley, 1989).

——, *et al.*, 'Personal Safety in Dangerous Places', *Journal of Contemporary Ethnography*, 21 (1992) 343–7.

WOLFGANG, M., *Patterns in Criminal Homicide* (Philadelphia: University of Pennsylvania Press, 1959).

WRIGHT, R., and DECKER, S., *Burglars on the Job: Street Life and Residential Break-ins* (Boston: North Eastern University Press, 1994).

Index

Printed in the United Kingdom
by Lightning Source UK Ltd.
102654UKS00001B/270

9 780198 258483